Bonhoeffer

An Introduction Through Drama

Tim Jorgenson

right © 2002 by Tim Jorgenson

Bonohoeffer
by Tim Jorgenson

Printed in the United States of America

Library of Congress Control Number: 2002116116
ISBN 1-591603-43-9

All rights reserved. No part of this publication may be reproduced or transmitted in any form or by any means without written permission of the publisher.

Unless otherwise indicated, Bible quotations are taken from the New Oxford Annotated Bible, Revised Standard Version. Copyright © 1962 by Oxford University Press: New York & Oxford.

Xulon Press
11350 Random Hills Road
Suite 800
Fairfax, VA 22030
(703) 279-6511
XulonPress.com

To order additional copies, call 1-866-909-BOOK (2665).

CAUTION: Professionals and amateurs are hereby warned that *Bonhoeffer* is subject to a royalty. It is fully protected under the copyright laws of the United States of America and of all countries with which the United States has reciprocal copyright relations. Any reading, book-club, or fellowship group having 20 members or less may perform public readings among its own members without having to obtain the consent of the author or his agent. All other rights, including professional, amateur, motion picture, recitation, lecturing, public reading, radio broadcasting, television, internet dissemination, print or electronic reproduction, and translation into foreign languages, are reserved. Permission to secure any of these rights must be made to the author's agent.

AUTHOR'S AGENT: All inquiries concerning rights should be addressed to the author's agent, at timjorg@gte.net.

**For Jean with special thanks to my parents,
Lillian and Howard**

BONHOEFFER:
A Play in Two Acts

DIETRICH BONHOEFFER (1906-1945)

Dietrich Bonhoeffer chose to serve the church, coming from a family whose members had made or were making distinguished careers in academia and the law. Despite growing up in a religiously tepid home, Dietrich became a leading Christian in his homeland. He earned a doctorate in theology by the age of 21. He was one of the first to identify Nazism as an enemy of Christianity. During the Hitler era, he cast his lot with the so-called "Confessing Church," which arose from within the State Church to stand apart from it. The Confessing Church embraced those Lutheran (Evangelical) congregations whose pastors, among other things, refused to take an oath to Adolf Hitler and who refused to ascribe to the so-called "Aryan Clause," which denied the possibility of Christianity to people of "Jewish blood."

During the 1930's Dietrich became involved in the international ecumenical movement, speaking with a voice at odds with the New Order in Germany. He developed extensive contacts abroad, especially in England and America, where he lived for a time. His vision, energy, and resourcefulness were vital to the running of clandestine Confessing seminaries in the '30's. Amidst the struggles of those years, Dietrich managed to publish several works, the most important being *Creation and Fall* (1932), *Cost of Discipleship* (1937), and *Life Together* (1938).

In 1939 he traveled to America in part at the urging of American friends. He could have accepted any of several academic or church posts in the United States. Instead, after a brief stay he returned to Germany, convinced that this was where God wished him to serve. After his return he not only served the Confessing Church but, unknown to that church, he became involved in a circle of the Resistance centered at the headquarters of German military intelligence. *Bonhoeffer* depicts the spiritual struggle that accompanied Dietrich in his journey to martyrdom.

BONHOEFFER: A Play in Two Acts

THE CHARACTERS

The directions for this play are cast with an eye to the economic dictates that govern most American, live theater. New plays and new playwrights, especially, are governed by the Casting Limit of Ten, if you will. This Limit prevails even at a time when the public has become accustomed to film and TV drama, whose offerings are afforded relatively large budgets. The live theater can hardly mimic these offerings, but only the misplaced vanity of greater age could blind the theater to the advisability of getting more mileage from the casts it uses.

Bonhoeffer employs 32 character roles. These roles are supportable by a cast as small as ten. Producers with the requisite resources are welcome to use larger casts, not to mention extras. Of use to spartan productions are the tables of characters that precede the two acts of this play. These tables show how ten actors, each identified by a number, can support the roles in the play. Additionally, the tables that follow list scenes in which each character appears.

Bonhoeffer

Cast List   Scenes   Description

The Bonhoeffer Family and Friends

Dietrich Bonhoeffer	All except 1A & 1E	A man in his late 30's already well known at home and abroad for his theological writings.
Mother [Paula Bonhoeffer]	1C; 1D; 1F; 2D	The intelligent, quietly devout, yet justifiably worried materfamilias of the Bonhoeffer brood.
Father [Karl Bonhoeffer]	1C; 1F	In his mid 70's, retired from a distinguished career as Germany's pre-eminent psychiatrist, Dietrich's father.
Karl-Frederich Bonhoeffer	1C; 1E; 1F	Dietrich's oldest brother, a physicist at the University of Leipzig.
Christine von Dohnanyi	1E; 1F	Dietrich's older sister, married to Hans von Dohnanyi.
Hans von Dohnanyi	1C	Served as a Supreme Court jurist before becoming chief counsel to the Abwehr.
Klaus	1E; 1F; 2J	Dietrich's somewhat older brother, a lawyer who worked for Lufthansa who became involved in a Resistance ring.
Uncle Paul von Hase	2G	A maternal uncle of Dietrich's; military commandant of Berlin.
Eberhard Bethge	1B; 1G; 2D; 2E	Dietrich's closest friend and a fellow Lutheran whom Dietrich met and taught whilst he (Dietrich) ran a clandestine seminary in Finkenwald, Germany.
Maria von Wedemeyer	2B; 2D; 2F	The bright-spirited, devout Prussian 18-year old fiancée of Dietrich.

Cast List · Scenes · Description

In State Service

Cast List	Scenes	Description
Ulrich Schmidt	1B; 1D; 2A; 2K; 2L	A man in his late 20's, a member of the Gestapo, who grew up in the blue-collar Wedding district of Berlin, where Dietrich once served as a pastor.
Group Leader Sonderkothen	2C; 2E; 2H; 2M	A well-educated young lawyer and member of the SS who is imbued with the modern perspective on life.
Corporal Andreas Rechter	2A; 2C; 2E; 2F; 2G	An Army man in his 20's, who befriends Dietrich.
Admiral Canaris	2I; 2K; 2M	Hitler's chief of the Abwehr, the military intelligence service, in his 60's.
Chanclry Rep	1F	An SS colonel from Hitler's Chancellery.
Chanclry Escort	1F	An SS lieutenant.
Tegel Sergeant	2F; 2G	An Army guard at Tegel prison.
Tegel Guard 1	2B; 2C; 2F	An Army guard at Tegel prison.
Tegel Guard 2	2H	An Army guard at Tegel prison.
RHSO Guard	2I; 2J	A guard in the Reich High Security Office prison.
Camp Guard 1	2K; 2L; 2M	An SS functionary at Flossenberg.
Camp Guard 2	2K; 2L; 2M	An SS functionary at Flossenberg.
Camp Guard 3	2L; 2M	An SS functionary at Flossenberg.
Camp Guard 4	2M	An SS functionary at Flossenberg.

Cast List	Scenes	Description

The British

Winston Churchill	1A	Prime Minister of Great Britain, 1940-1945.
Anthony Eden	1A	Foreign Secretary in Winston Churchill's wartime government.
Secretary 1	1A	On the staff of Churchill.
Serectary 2	1A	On the staff of Churchill.

Others

Patron M	1B	A man.
Patron F	1B	A woman.
Waitress	1B	Serving at a restaurant in Berlin.
Lady	1B	A woman that Dietrich hoped to marry who rejected him.

Extra, non-speaking characters may be added to the scenes, as described in the play.

THE SET

Bonhoeffer is supportable by a simple set, where props, sounds, lighting, costumes, and limited scenery can provide the settings for the actions of the play. A set with two tiers rising towards the backstage will do. The tiers should be connected with one another and with the stage by flights of steps on stage right and stage left. Additional direction is provided within the text of the acts.

ACTS AND SCENES

There are two acts, with 7 scenes in the first act and 13 in the second.

BONHOEFFER: Act 1

Boldface characters listed below appear in both acts, plain-text characters in Act 1 only, and *italicized* in Act 2 only.

	ACT 1 SCENE:	A	B	C	D	E	F	G
1	**Dietrich**		B	C	D		F	G
2	**Eberhard**		B					G
2	*Camp Guard 1*							
3	**Ulrich**		B		D			
3	Chanclry Escort						F	
3	*Tegel Guard 1*							
3	*Tegel Guard 2*							
4	**Karl-Frederich**			C		E	F	
4	Eden	A						
4	*Uncle Paul*							
4	*RHSO Guard*							
4	*Camp Guard 2*							
5	**Klaus**					E	F	
5	Dohnanyi			C				
5	*Sonderkothen*							
6	**Father**			C			F	
6	Churchill	A						
6	*Canaris*							
6	*Tegel Sergeant*							
7	**Mother**			C	D		F	
7	Secretary 1	A						
7	Patron F		B					
7	*Camp Guard 3*							
8	**Christine**					E	F	
8	Lady		B					
8	*Camp Guard 4*							
9	*Maria*							
9	Secretary 2	A						
9	Waitress		B					
10	*Rechter*							
10	Chanclry Rep						F	
10	Patron M		B					

SCENE 1A

<u>SETTING</u>:

WE ARE IN THE WARTIME, BUNKER OFFICE OF WINSTON CHURCHILL IN JULY 1942. THERE IS NO EXTERIOR LIGHT EVIDENT. THE OFFICE MAY BE MERELY SUGGESTED OR IT MAY BE FURNISHED WITH SOMBER, LEATHER-CLAD PLUSH ARMCHAIRS THAT BEFIT A WARTIME LEADER.

<u>AT RISE</u>:

AS THE LIGHTS COME UP WE SEE CHURCHILL PACING, CLUTCHING NEWS CLIPPINGS AND PAPERS. SECRETARY 1 HOLDS A CLIPBOARD WITH A SHEAF OF PAPERS AFFIXED.

CHURCHILL

What I want to know is who the devil this Dietrich Bonhoeffer is.

SECRETARY 1

I'll have them look for more articles, sir.

CHURCHILL

I've read enough. I've got plenty of facts. It's not the sort of thing you can pick out from a file. What I don't yet see is the heart of this man. What motivates him?

SECRETARY 2 ENTERS.

SECRETARY 2

Mr Eden is here.

CHURCHILL

Is he a cowardly opportunist or a brave patriot?

SECRETARY 2

Mr Churchill, the Foreign Secretary is here.

CHURCHILL

Yes, I heard. Send him in.

SECRETARY 2

Yes, sir. Should I hold off on the new de-crypts?

CHURCHILL

I'll dig through them later.

SECRETARY 2

Yes, sir.

SECRETARY 2 EXITS.

SECRETARY 1

Perhaps he—Pastor Bonhoeffer—is something else.

CHURCHILL

Yes, perhaps. But I must look at him with the business of state in mind.

SECRETARY 1

I don't know what he is but I don't think he's a coward.

CHURCHILL

For his sake, I hope you're right. Well, that'll be all.

SECRETARY 1

Yes, sir.

SECRETARY 1 EXITS. EDEN ENTERS.

EDEN

Winston.

CHURCHILL

My Dear Eden, you've prepared a reply along the lines we discussed earlier today?

EDEN

I have. Are you having second thoughts? I thought we'd agreed on what I was to say.

CHURCHILL

I know. but let's hear it. I want to hear it.

EDEN

Yes.

(READING FROM A LETTER HE HOLDS IN HAND)
My dear Bishop.

CHURCHILL
My dear Bishop Bell.

EDEN
(OVERLAPPING)
Just "dear Bishop" but of course George Bell.

CHURCHILL
More "thorn" than "bell." Read on.

EDEN
(READING)
When you visited me on 30 June, you were kind enough to let me have a memorandum on your talk with two German pastors whom you had met in Stockholm at the end of May, together with a report on a statement by one of the pastors.

Those interesting documents have by now been carefully examined. Without challenging the honest conviction of your informers in the least, I have no doubt that it would be contrary to the interest of our nation to provide them with any answer whatever. I know well that this decision will be somewhat disappointing to you. But in view of the delicate circumstances connected with it, I cannot do other than ask you to accept it, something that you will surely understand.

CHURCHILL
Maybe.

EDEN
(READING)
Sincerely Yours, Anthony Eden.

(LOOKING UP)
Well, what are your second thoughts?

CHURCHILL

What do you know about this Bonhoeffer, the one who prepared the statement given to our dear Bishop Bell? Do you or I have any idea about what makes him tick?

EDEN

How do we ever know what makes a person tick? Anyway, we're at war.

CHURCHILL

I want to know whether this Bonhoeffer is someone I ought to admire. I have the nagging feeling that perhaps we should help him and his ring of conspirators.

EDEN

He—and they—would be another hobby when the nation can ill afford another hobby. Please, Mr Prime Minister, don't even think of it.

CHURCHILL

This is not a hobby. In war you pay attention to your friends as well as your enemies.

EDEN

Indeed. And how would our friends the Russians and the Americans view our attending to the likes of Bonhoeffer and his co-conspirators?

CHURCHILL

If dealing with a German resistance helps shorten the war, why should they complain?

EDEN

It depends on the terms that end the war.

CHURCHILL

Well, the Americans have just begun and they insist on unconditional surrender.

EDEN

Exactly. And the Russians—quite simply—want to smash the Germans in the face, so they'll not tolerate any diplomatic parleys.

CHURCHILL

Talk doesn't have to be diplomatic. It can be surreptitious.

EDEN

Neither the Russians nor the Americans would be pleased if they found out—and they would eventually.

CHURCHILL

Perhaps, but we dare not fight so hard we lose our consciences. We fight for a noble cause—for freedom and human dignity. Let's not forget that because that cause transcends borders.

EDEN

Don't be trapped by your eloquence, Winston. Ours is a noble cause because we are a free people who do not wish to be enslaved. The Germans, on the other hand, are an enslaved people who have become accustomed to their yoke, albeit some are beginning to notice the yoke cuts a lot of blood.

CHURCHILL

So you believe the German resistance is merely pragmatic, wanting to stem the flow of blood that Herr Hitler revels in.

EDEN

I think that's what it amounts to.

CHURCHILL

Then how do you account for the participation of these pastors—that's what's bothered me since we talked earlier. Especially what about this Bonhoeffer? Why would he have chosen to return to Germany from the States just as the war was about to begin—despite a career of excoriating the Nazis at home and abroad?

EDEN

You feel a kinship.

CHURCHILL

That's not the point. We've stubbed our toe on a German resistance group that includes the likes of a Bonhoeffer. What does it mean? Is he a mere showpiece or an indication of the integrity of the resistance? If they are opportunists, I wouldn't want them in power at war's end. But if they are true patriots they'll care less about their own power and more about preserving whatever's good in Germany.

EDEN

I thought you thought there was little good to start with in Germany—aside from the music and science. Anyway, we simply can't think of dealings with *any* German resistance—not right now, not if we keep our allies in mind.

CHURCHILL

Allies and friends aren't the same thing. The German resistance may—just may—be worthy of our friendship and support, even if they can't be allies.

EDEN

I've no doubt they wish to staunch the flow of blood. That's commendable, more commendable than the blood lust of Hitler and his gang. But so what? What else do they think? What's their objective? Who knows? And no one of us should care. What this resistance group thinks is irrelevant. We can't begin to deal with them because we can't even suggest to any Germans that they will have any say-so whatsoever in the terms of a surrender. You've made your place by reminding everyone of the harsh fact we must fight Germany till we've finished them on *our* terms.

CHURCHILL

I wouldn't be so sure I've made my place. I'll have no place in any history I'd want to read if we don't win this fight—but we're fighting for a decent civilization, not merely for power.

EDEN

Is Stalin fighting for civilization?

CHURCHILL

He fights for power.

EDEN

Precisely. This is a conflict of powers.

CHURCHILL

Dictatorships always reduce everything to matters of power.

EDEN

Civilizations in conflict reduce matters to power.

CHURCHILL

If that were true we'd all be deserving of pity. I thank God I was born in a country where power and pity aren't the only scales in the balance of discernment.

EDEN

Right now they may be the only scales we dare touch and of the two pity should be the least of our concerns. We can't talk to the German resistance out of pity.

CHURCHILL

I would never suggest as much. There are allies of convenience and allies of substance. We can't afford the German resistance for convenience. But can we afford to ignore their substance?

EDEN

We can't afford them at all. We've little to gain and two key allies to perturb. It's as simple as that.

CHURCHILL

You've always had a practical outlook. But if we were merely practical perhaps we'd long ago have surrendered to the Nazis. However crazy, I believe it's simply not right to surrender our homes and our freedom to the tyranny of madmen.

EDEN

I don't disagree. But defending one's home and defending freedom are two quite different things. To defend our homes we may have to ally ourselves with tyrants.

CHURCHILL

Yes, which is why we should give pause when we come across decent people who like us seem motivated by more than mere considerations of power and opportunity. Islands of civilization must be allied in this dark world, otherwise we shall all sink.

EDEN
Then let the German resistance be its own fighting island.

CHURCHILL
The road from mere practicality to mere mockery is short.

EDEN
Pardon me, Winston, but only time will tell whether the German resistance is noble or opportunistic. When that happens, it will be too late to affect the outcome of the war. We cannot aid that resistance. We can't even talk to them.

(PAUSE)
I should send this letter as written. Do you agree?

CHURCHILL
As written, the letter practically sends itself and our national circumstance seals it, I regretfully admit.

EDEN
There's nothing more to be said.

CHURCHILL
There's always more to be said, but God has the last word.

EDEN
Then we shall leave Bonhoeffer and his likes to God.

(PAUSE)

CHURCHILL
Yes, may God have mercy on them.

EDEN (HOLDING UP THE LETTER)
With your permission, Mr Prime Minister, I'll be on my way and so will this.

CHURCHILL
Yes, yes, yes. Be on your way, my dear Eden. Thank you for indulging me in this matter.

EDEN
You took a greater interest than I would have expected.

CHURCHILL
To no telling effect. Good evening.

EDEN
Good evening, Winston.

CHURCHILL NODS. EDEN EXITS.

CHURCHILL
(SPEAKING INTO AN INTERCOM OR BELLOWING)
Ladies, send in the de-crypts.

**CHURCHILL RESUMES HIS READING
AND PACING. THE LIGHTS GO DIM
ON THE SET. CHURCHILL EXITS.**

SCENE 1B

SETTING:

AN UNDER-POPULATED OUTDOOR BIER-GARTEN IN BERLIN, LATE SUMMER 1942.

AT RISE:

STREET NOISES ARE HEARD AS THE LIGHTS COME UP. DIETRICH AND LADY ARE SEEN SEATED AT STAGE RIGHT. SEATED AT STAGE LEFT PATRONS F AND M ARE A DATING COUPLE, LARGELY OBLIVIOUS TO ANYTHING BUT THEMSELVES. DIETRICH AND THE LADY ARISE. DIETRICH BEGINS TO EMBRACE LADY BUT SHE RAISES A HAND AND HE STOPS. SHE PUTS THAT HAND TO HER MOUTH, BLOWS DIETRICH A KISS, THEN ABRUPTLY EXITS. DIETRICH RESUMES HIS SEAT. EBERHARD ENTERS STAGE OPPOSITE THE LADY'S EXIT.

EBERHARD

I thought she...

DIETRICH
She didn't want to see you. It was hard enough, she said, to see me. And I'd hoped we could at least talk.

EBERHARD
It's been some time since you broke up.

DIETRICH
We've been writing recently. I thought we could have a conversation. I thought your presence here would put her more at ease. But it was not to be. Please, have a seat.

EBERHARD
(SITTING)
I think you'd better give up.

WAITRESS ENTERS.

WAITRESS
Would you gentlemen like a drink?

DIETRICH
Eberhard?

EBERHARD
Certainly.

DIETRICH
Two Paulis, please.

WAITRESS
Yes, sir.

WAITRESS EXITS.

DIETRICH
She could never stomach my extra-curricular associations and activities.

EBERHARD
I thought she hated the Party.

DIETRICH
I know we're almost alone out here, but let's call them, as we usually do, the Modernists. Yes, she hates the Modernists—but she fears all that means.

EBERHARD
She wouldn't have to fear being around you, except for your zeal. Angels seem to manage your survival.

DIETRICH
Let angels be angels. It's our job as mortals to make choices. She has made hers and I make mine. I guess I must live with hers. And soon I will have to live with your choice.

EBERHARD
You mean about marrying Renaté?

DIETRICH
I'm not thinking about my niece and you. Whether you two choose to marry is for you and her to decide. No, I'm thinking of your role in the state, specifically in the Army.

EBERHARD
I will serve when I'm called up.

WAITRESS ENTERS WITH A TRAY BEAR-
ING TWO GLASSES OF BEER.

DIETRICH

(SPEAKING TO THE WAITRESS)
Thank you.

DIETRICH PAYS THE WAITRESS
FOR THE BEERS, WHICH SHE
SETS OUT FOR THE TWO.

DIETRICH
Thank you.

WAITRESS
You're welcome.
WAITRESS EXITS.

DIETRICH
(IN A WHISPER)
I don't want you to serve in the Army. Here's to staying
out of the Army!

EBERHARD
That won't be possible. But I'll drink to it anyway. I'm
thirsty and Germany is now a suburb of hell.

DIETRICH
I'm grateful to God I'm able to be in this hell with the best
of friends.

EBERHARD
Here's a toast to friendship!

BOTH

Prosit.

DIETRICH

Let's think how we can keep you out of the Army.

DIETRICH AND EBERHARD SIP THEIR BEERS FROM TIME TO TIME DURING THE FOLLOWING DIALOGUE.

EBERHARD

That would be a waste of time. I don't have the connections you have. And anyway, you're able to stay out of the Army because in a manner of speaking you're already in the Army.

DIETRICH

We must be careful.

EBERHARD

I don't share that with anyone. It's a fact, though. Your affiliation with the Abwehr has saved your skin.

DIETRICH

But sadly only a few others.

EBERHARD

A few saved are better than none at all.

DIETRICH

There are more and more Jewish persons disappearing every day. We've got to do something different. I told George Bell about this situation when I saw him in Sweden. The only real hope is to change the government...

EBERHARD
(OVERLAPPING)
Now I'm the one who must suggest care.

DIETRICH
That couple back there isn't interested in us...but, I agree, we don't want to get into bad habits. We'll talk of "therapy," as we have on other occasions.

EBERHARD
The Modernists despise therapy.

(PAUSE)
Have you heard back from the Bishop?

DIETRICH
Nothing. We've been in contact with our representative in Switzerland. But we've heard nothing.

EBERHARD
Then you *have* heard something. No answer amounts to an answer of no interest.

DIETRICH
I hate to admit it.

EBERHARD
The bishop's reply—or non-reply—only strengthens my resolve. We Germans can expect no help from abroad. I will do nothing to actively assist the Modernists, but I will do nothing to resist Army service. To do otherwise is to invite death.

DIETRICH
Serve as a pastor in the Army.

ULRICH ENTERS, DRESSED IN A SUIT.
DIETRICH NOTICES.

EBERHARD
You know that's impossible.

DIETRICH
(SPEAKING STAGILY, AS A CUE TO EBERHARD)
In Leipzig there's a marvelous exhibit deploring decadent art.

EBERHARD
(CLUED IN)
Yes, so I've heard.

ULRICH APPROACHES THE TWO.

DIETRICH
(STANDING)
I recognize you.

ULRICH
Pastor Bonhoeffer.

DIETRICH
From where, where...?

ULRICH
From your confirmation class in the Wedding district, Berlin, 1932.

DIETRICH
Ten years ago! Don't tell me.

ULRICH

I've changed a lot since then but I'm still what you'd call a rebel.

DIETRICH
(EXTENDING HIS HAND)

Ulrich Schmidt. Ullie...come here, come here.

ULRICH AND DIETRICH SHAKE HANDS.

DIETRICH

Let me introduce you to my good friend, Eberhard Bethge. Eberhard, this is Ulrich Schmidt, a former confirmation student of mine...

ULRICH

A confirmand never confirmed.

DIETRICH

Not yet, at least.

ULRICH AND EBERHARD SHAKE HANDS
AND EXCHANGE GREETINGS.

DIETRICH

You were the brightest boy in any of my confirmation classes and...

(NOTICING ULRICH'S NAZI PARTY PIN)

you now are no longer a boy, of course, but a modern man.

EBERHARD
A Modernist.

ULRICH
So you do remember?

DIETRICH
Yes. How could I forget? I don't suppose you've left your agnosticism behind.

ULRICH
(SHRUGGING)
If God exists he doesn't make Himself personally evident. I've come to believe in a Creative Principle; call it "God" if you want. But in this life, I'm convinced, we're left on our own.

DIETRICH
What of the Word of God? What of Christ? What more disclosure could you want? There is enough there to return love for love.

ULRICH
That is the talk of a theologian, not of someone who's had to live life as an ordinary person.

DIETRICH
(PULLING OVER A NEARBY CHAIR)
Did you have to join *them?* Take a seat. Please join us.

PATRON M AND PATRON F ARISE.
THEY EXIT WHILE ULRICH
SAYS THE FOLLOWING.

ULRICH
(REMAINING STANDING)
I didn't have to. I wanted to. The New Leadership restored hope and dignity to working people. In Wedding there's been plenty of work to do these years of the Leader. And the indignities of the Versailles agreement have been buried in our nation's triumphs.

DIETRICH
There was too much vengeance in the Versailles agreement.

EBERHARD
I'll say.

DIETRICH
When, of course, vengeance must be left to God.

ULRICH
Isn't that being irresponsible, as you would say?

DIETRICH
It's being very responsible...to God.

ULRICH
But what about us mere mortals? Would it have been responsible for Germans to let the Versailles agreement stand?

DIETRICH
No. We had every obligation to ourselves and to justice to work for its change but not by invading our neighbors.

ULRICH
You should watch what you say.

WAITRESS ENTERS. DIETRICH
SIGNALS HER TO COME OVER.
SHE COMES UP TO DIETRICH.

DIETRICH
(TO ULRICH)
Would you join us in a St Pauli? Or perhaps something else.

ULRICH
I don't think I should linger.

DIETRICH
Please...to celebrate acquaintance renewed.

ULRICH
All right.

DIETRICH
(TO THE WAITRESS)
Good, a St Pauli for our guest, please.

WAITRESS
Yes, sir.

WAITRESS EXITS.

DIETRICH
(TOUCHING THE CHAIR
HE HAD PULLED OVER EARLIER)
Here, take this.

ULRICH TAKES THE CHAIR AND
SEATS HIMSELF BETWEEN
DIETRICH AND EBERHARD.

EBERHARD
Mr Schmidt, what do you do now?

EBERHARD
I'm with the Gestapo.

DIETRICH
Yes, they do have bright people there.

ULRICH
Pastor, I had heard you were in New York three years ago.
You should have stayed there.

DIETRICH
Thank you, but I had to return.

ULRICH
But your views! You're with the Confessing Church, such
as it is, aren't you?

DIETRICH
I have no choice.

ULRICH
We're not living in medieval times. You do have a choice.
Take some friendly advice, your association with the military intelligence service will only protect you to a point. You
need to become much more enthusiastic about the Leader
and the Party. I'm surprised the Abwehr continues to use
you.

DIETRICH

I have my uses.

WAITRESS ENTERS WITH A GLASS OF
BEER, WHICH SHE SETS BEFORE ULRICH.
DIETRICH PAYS AS ULRICH SPEAKS.

ULRICH

The Party would find you even more useful if you were to cease working for the Abwehr and sign up to serve in the uniformed Army.

WAITRESS EXITS.

DIETRICH

I'll gladly serve as a pastor in the Army.

ULRICH

You know that's not possible. The Confessing Church is illegal; your pastorate is illegal. You should join the State Church.

DIETRICH

Any pastor who takes an oath to Adolf Hitler has betrayed the Living God.

EBERHARD

Dietrich!

ULRICH
(OVERLAPPING)

You shouldn't have returned to Germany! Troublemakers and other misfits will only be put away, as our Leader has promised. You can rely on his promises, Pastor.

DIETRICH

I do not doubt them. We see the results. But we would all be better off if we lived—or attempted to live—lives in obedience to God.

ULRICH

You should obey what you can see and hear. I obey a man who has restored greatness to Germany.

DIETRICH

So it may seem.

ULRICH

You must watch what you say.

EBERHARD

Let's drink to a wholesome Germany.

ULRICH
(RAISING HIS GLASS)

A wholesome Germany will be a cleansed Germany. To a wholesome Germany!

DIETRICH
(RAISING HIS GLASS)

To a Germany renewed in the true Lord of us all.

EBERHARD AND DIETRICH SIP
THEIR BEERS. ULRICH DRINKS
MOST IF NOT ALL OF HIS GLASS.

ULRICH

God doesn't renew societies. Keeping religion private has had the advantage of bringing peace to modern society. The last thing we need are more religious wars.

DIETRICH

I yearn for peace, but war isn't the worst fear. More to be feared than war itself is serving false gods.

ULRICH

I must go.

DIETRICH

I'm disappointed you have joined the Party but delighted God has given us this opportunity to meet again.

ULRICH
(STANDING)

You have been candid. Let me be candid. I shouldn't be associating with you. Anyway I must be off to check on my wife at the hospital.

DIETRICH
(STANDING)

You're married! And I didn't even ask. Congratulations! But is she ill?

ULRICH

My wife's not ill; she's due to deliver at any time.

EBERHARD

Best wishes to you and your wife.

DIETRICH

May God bless you both and your child.

EBERHARD
(STANDING)
Let's drink to a successful delivery and a healthy child!

ULRICH
I'll drink to that.

ALL
(GRABBING AND CLINKING THEIR GLASSES,
THEN DRINKING)
Prosit!

ULRICH
And now I must go. A pleasure to meet you, Mr Bethge. Pastor, if you come around to the State Church point of view we can talk again.

DIETRICH
I understand.

ULRICH
Good day!

ULRICH EXITS QUICKLY.

DIETRICH
What a curse!

EBERHARD
What do you mean?

DIETRICH
(SITTING)
The brokenness in this world. Thank heavens, sin has not

broken God's will to sustain and regain us. He has a purpose for us in life.

(PAUSE)

I can't understand how Ulrich could have joined...

EBERHARD
(SITTING)

Like others, he sees good in the Modernists.

DIETRICH

Yes, yes, the worst sort of evil is the kind cloaked in good, though the good becomes less and the evil more evident with each passing day.

EBERHARD

You were cordial enough just now.

DIETRICH

Because God commands hospitality.

EBERHARD

I was surprised Mr Schmidt knew of your Abwehr association.

DIETRICH

That's no surprise. Within the security apparatus it must be common knowledge.

EBERHARD

That common! You must become more discreet about your expressions against the Modernists. That even Mr Schmidt knew of your Abwehr status suggests you are being widely talked about—and probably observed.

DIETRICH

Perhaps he merely takes a personal interest in me. Anyway, I can't change myself to save myself—what will I have gained? I cannot love my neighbor, as Christ commands, and abide what the Leader and Party are doing to people in this country, not to mention to Europe.

EBERHARD

You not only disagree with the Modernists, you declare war.

DIETRICH

I declare "therapy."

EBERHARD

I can't see the warrant in that. Rather than that, Jesus Christ went to the cross.

DIETRICH

As God willed it. But for us now I think God wills something different. We must fight the evil that seeks to kill our neighbors and the neighbors of Germany.

EBERHARD

Resistance, yes, but I can't see that God wants pastors serving in efforts to overthrow the government, as evil as it most surely is. Let God in His time bring that about.

DIETRICH

So you pray for its demise?

EBERHARD

You know I do.

DIETRICH

But don't you see the inconsistency?

EBERHARD

Between praying for the fall and actually having a hand in it?

DIETRICH

Yes.

DIETRICH TAKES OUT A PIPE AND FIDDLES WITH IT DURING THE FOLLOWING, PREPARATORY TO LIGHTING THE PIPE.

EBERHARD

You and I have committed ourselves to being pastors of the faithful. *They* are our first priority.

DIETRICH
(WHISPERING)

And that may mean we must be the first to declare "therapy."

EBERHARD
(WHISPERING)

It's quite one thing to save Jews and Gypsies from depraved actions—quite another to conduct lethal therapy on a government. I've yet to be convinced.

DIETRICH

I must convince you. Saving and overthrowing are deeply linked now in our homeland.

EBERHARD

You don't give up. Perhaps this zeal is what frightens women away.

DIETRICH

You think so?

EBERHARD

I've wondered. If you keep this up you're going to get yourself killed. And for what good? Save yourself for the church, for the faithful.

DIETRICH

I will let Jesus Christ do the saving, thank you.

EBERHARD

At least be prudent. Mr Schmidt suggested you shouldn't have returned. He may be aware of increased surveillance of your activities.

DIETRICH

That doesn't change a thing. In a few days I travel to Prussia. The Gestapo will loose track of me. I'm a small fish in their big pond.

EBERHARD

It's all well and good to go to Prussia for the sake of the faithful. You're fulfilling your pastoral duties. But for heaven's sake, stop thinking you are personally obliged to participate in efforts at "therapy." That is prideful foolishness.

DIETRICH

Forgive me if I have been proud, Eberhard, but I assure you I do everything to avoid common foolishness. I'm simply trying to do my duty, not only as a pastor, but as a Christian. Our duty as Christians is to God and our neighbors. What else would Christ have us live for?

EBERHARD
How about the blessings of an ordinary, Godly life?

AS DIETRICH LIGHTS HIS PIPE
THE LIGHTS GO OUT ON THE SET.

DIETRICH AND EBERHARD EXIT.

SCENE 1C

SETTING:

WE ARE AT FRIEDERICHSBRUNN, THE BON-HOEFFER FAMILY RETREAT IN THE HARZ MOUNTAINS ON A COOL, SUNNY MORNING IN AUTUMN 1942. TO ONE SIDE OF THE STAGE THERE IS A RUGGED TABLE WITH CHAIRS AND SOME POTTED GERANIUMS. A RADIO SET, WITH AN ANTENNA, SITS ON THE TABLE. THE DOOR TO A KITCHEN MAY BE IMAGINED TO BE JUST OFFSTAGE.

AT RISE:

AS THE LIGHTS COME UP WE HEAR THE TWITTER OF BIRDS. FATHER IS FIDDLING WITH THE RADIO. MOTHER ENTERS WITH TWO CUPS OF COFFEE. SHE SETS THE CUPS OF COFFEE ON THE TABLE, THEN TAKES A SEAT ACROSS FROM FATHER. MOTHER AND FATHER TAKE SIPS OF COFFEE FROM TIME TO TIME DURING THE FOLLOWING.

FATHER

How's Dietrich this morning? He should get up and enjoy this autumn air.

MOTHER

ne's feeling better. He's always helped by home cooking, Papa. You know I'd feel better if you had that back in the attic.

FATHER

I wanted to see if we'd get better reception out here. For some reason it's been hard to pick up the BBC lately.

MOTHER

Papa, are you listening for our sake or the boys'? I'm sure they're happy to forget about the war and about the government.

FATHER

Don't worry. I'm keeping a distance.

KARL-FREDERICH ENTERS. HE AND FATHER EXCHANGE NODS AS HE WALKS TO MOTHER AND GIVES HER A KISS ON THE CHEEK.

KARL-FREDERICH

Good morning. Mama. Papa, what are you trying to do?

FATHER

I want to get London on the radio.

KARL-FREDERICH

You're not having problems in picking up nearby stations?

FATHER

No.

KARL-FREDERICH

We need to work on the antenna. Here, let me work at that thing.

KARL-FREDERICH WALKS AROUND THE
TABLE FROM MOTHER TO FATHER AND
BEGINS REFORMING THE ANTENNA INTO
A CIRCULAR ARRANGEMENT.

FATHER

Leave it to the physicist!

DOHNANYI ENTERS, WHILE KARL
-FREDERICH CONTINUES TO FIDDLE
WITH THE RADIO.

DOHNANYI

Good morning, Mama, Papa.

FATHER AND MOTHER

Good morning, Hans.

KARL-FREDERICH
(OVERLAPPING)

Morning, Hans.

DOHNANYI

Looks like we have a little clandestine activity going on.

KARL-FREDERICH
Just physics, Hans. Just physics.

DOHNANYI
It's good there's at least one innocent in this family.

MOTHER
He's innocent only by degrees but I say and say again, we must be careful.

DOHNANYI
Up here in the mountains we can all afford to breathe easier. We can hope that someday that becomes possible throughout Germany and Europe.

KARL-FREDERICH
We'll have a lot of air pollution to take care of first.

FATHER
Always the physicist.

DIETRICH ENTERS.

DIETRICH
Good morning, Mama, Papa, Hans, Karl-Frederich.

FATHER, MOTHER, DOHNANYI, KARL-FREDERICH BID DIETRICH "GOOD MORNING" "GREETINGS", ETC. DIETRICH KISSES MOTHER.

KARL-FREDERICH
We should be able to get the BBC now.

BBC RADIO VOICE
…the continued bombing of Hamburg. In news from the Russian Front, there are reports from our Soviet allies of a growing battle for the control of Stalingrad, on the Volga River. Despite heavy casualties, Soviet authorities are rushing reinforcements to hold this key industrial city against the German 6th Army. In the Pacific Theatre American authorities report a battle at Cape Esperance near Guadalcanal. The sinking of one Japanese cruiser is reported. Elsewhere…

MOTHER
(OVERLAPPING THE LAST)
Enough, enough.

KARL-FREDERICH
TURNS OFF THE RADIO.

MOTHER
We came here to get away from all that. Papa, if you want to listen, you'll have to take the radio up into the attic. Karl-Frederich, make sure your father hides it well.

DIETRICH
Have the police been up here, even?

FATHER
It's only a matter of time. The local Party leader has taken on the task of coordinating the inspection of every house. Karl-Frederich, let's take this up.

MOTHER

Breakfast will be ready in about 20 minutes. I'm not going up there to summon you two.

FATHER

Of course, Mama.

FATHER AND KARL-FREDERICH EXIT, CARRYING THE RADIO AND RELEVANT APPARATUS.

DIETRICH

Mother, Hans wanted to take a brief walk in the woods. If you don't mind?

MOTHER

No, but if you come back late don't expect a warm breakfast.

DIETRICH

Hot or cold, I'm sure it will be good.

MOTHER

Save the goodwill for the pulpit. You know what I mean.

DIETRICH

I know. We'll keep our walk brief.

MOTHER EXITS. DIETRICH AND DOHNANYI BEGIN THEIR "WALK," AS MUCH AS THE SET WILL PERMIT.

DIETRICH

Beautiful morning, isn't it?

DOHNANYI

It is but I want to get right to the point, so we can enjoy our walk.

DIETRICH

Yes, what's this secret business we must discuss, Hans? When I come to Friederichsbrunn I try to forget the war, politics, the Modernists.

DOHNANYI

Planning has intensified for the assassination attempt.

DIETRICH

It has? When I met Bishop Bell in Sweden I reported planning was already underway.

DOHNANYI

Well it now includes additional resistance circles. It's becoming quite serious and we're becoming more thorough.

DIETRICH

I put the best face on this endeavor when I met with George in Sweden. I hope this time the endeavor meets with success. How many efforts have there been?

DOHNANYI

At least two dozen, if not more. We must keep trying.

DIETRICH

I agree. I've been wanting to ask you. What does our boss, Admiral Canaris, think of yet another attempt on the Leader?

DOHNANYI

He isn't directly involved.

DIETRICH

In the Third Reich if he knows of it, he's involved.

DOHNANYI

He doesn't know of it yet.

(PAUSE)

But if he knew of it he'd approve...I think.

DIETRICH

You're not sure.

DOHNANYI

He's always been a puzzle. For one thing he wouldn't be where he is today if it weren't for Hitler. But for all that, I know he doesn't like Hitler or the Hitler crowd. While he knows what some of us in the Abwehr are doing and even helps us on occasion—as when he approved your employment by the Abwehr—he doesn't seem prepared to participate in Hitler's removal. He's not the spider building the web; he's the spider that lets others do it for him.

DIETRICH

He's half-animated to revolt.

DOHNANYI

That's putting it nicely.

DIETRICH

The politics of half measures.

DOHNANYI
So many like half measures, Dietrich. While keeping themselves out of danger they salve their consciences.

DIETRICH
A paralysis of modern man I'm very familiar with.

DOHNANYI
You think that's a peculiarity of our times?

DIETRICH
Not the half measures, but the inability to see that obedience to Jesus Christ demands full measures.

DOHNANYI
I'm not sure that's a peculiarity of our times. More pertinent right now is whether you're willing to continue helping the Resistance—perhaps in ways other than being a messenger.

DIETRICH
You raise a touchy question, one that many of us in the church must ask again and again. Just how far should our resistance to an oppressive and evil state go? My dear Eberhard—you know him—

DOHNANYI
(OVERLAPPING)
Pastor Bethge, of course, I remember him.

DIETRICH
Eberhard is pursuing the line of passive resistance. He's not convinced there is Biblical warrant to actively participate in the overthrow of a government. Yet he is sympathetic to the overthrow of *this* government.

DOHNANYI

What about you? You've acted as a messenger. Will you also pray for the assassination effort? Can you? That would mean a lot to the men and women involved, if they knew you were praying for our endeavor.

DIETRICH

Is that what this walk is about?

DOHNANYI

Nothing less.

DIETRICH

Is it *I* that would be the comfort? Or that a prayer of this nature is laid before God?

DOHNANYI

Maybe both. None of us is a theologian. And few if any would consider themselves religious.

DIETRICH

Yet this would mean something to them—to the others, I mean?

DOHNANYI

Yes, and to me.

DIETRICH

I shouldn't be so certain my prayers are so powerful or that this one would be worthy to lay before the Lord God. Even I wonder at times.

DOHNANYI

How can you consider participating in this plot yet not pray to God about it? You must have. You've made a point—

and just suggested—that those who commit to Christ must entirely commit to His service.

DIETRICH

Not only to His service, but to His kingdom. The markers of His kingdom are faith, hope, and love. If I take up the sword, as I have, it must be for the love of others and in reliance on God's mercy. I believe the struggle against Hitler is part of God's story in our time, but God is the author and the final editor.

DOHNANYI

What are you?

DIETRICH

I struggle to know. Sometimes I think I'm a printer's devil, of no use to God and of little value to even those I purport to serve.

DOHNANYI

Others don't see you that way.

DIETRICH

They have not the eyes of God. Even amidst my pastoral work, perhaps especially in that work, I also find myself thinking of having a wife and family. Indeed...

DOHNANYI

I doubt that God condemns you for that. He made you a man.

DIETRICH

It's not that. It's not that. It's my desire to escape from the struggle, to have what we could call a normal existence.

DOHNANYI

I would like to have one, too. I find nothing wrong with wanting a normal existence.

DIETRICH

Yes, as God created us. But because of the Fall we can't rely on the normal to be normative. Christ challenges the normal. His norm was and is the cross. More often than you realize, I don't wish to take up the cross.

DOHNANYI

Does participating in this assassination mean taking up your cross or turning away from it?

DIETRICH

You are asking the terrible question.

DOHNANYI

I'm asking as a brother-in-law...

DIETRICH

I regard you as a brother. You're bringing me into the Abwehr has allowed me to continue my work for the Confessing Church. Otherwise the Gestapo would have already cooked me.

DOHNANYI

Yes.

DIETRICH

I *do* pray for the downfall of this government. No government is perfect but this government is almost entirely at odds with the Kingdom of God. It must fall.

DOHNANYI

And Hitler?

DIETRICH

God will in His good time bring judgement and justice, as He always does. I can't be sure a successful assassination is part of God's plan, but I am sure as a disciple of Christ I must be willing to give up my life and my reputation for Christ's sake.

DOHNANYI

That's what I wanted to hear. You will pray for us, won't you?

(PAUSE)
DIETRICH

Yes, I will, for I believe the removal of the Party from power is part of God's plan and I can hope that he blesses our swords in that task. I see no other way we Germans can take responsibility for the evil that engulfs us and others.

THE COO OF A
MOURNING DOVE IS HEARD.

DOHNANYI

What was that?

DIETRICH

A mourning dove.

THE COO OF THE MOURNING DOVE
IS HEARD AGAIN.

DIETRICH
Do you know what that means?

DOHNANYI
No. What does it mean?

DIETRICH
In the local folklore they say the first person you see on a sunny morning after hearing a mourning dove in the woods is a person destined for a long journey.

DOHNANYI
I didn't know you had an interest in folklore.

DIETRICH
I sometimes think the Holy Spirit speaks through folklore...and, as folklore would have it, through the natural realm.

DOHNANYI
How can you tell when God is really speaking?

DIETRICH
You see whether or not God is speaking by looking through the lens of the crucifixion and resurrection of Jesus Christ.

DOHNANYI
You mix metaphors. Anyway my lens is dirty.

DIETRICH
Everyone's lens is splattered with clay and yet, God willing, we can hear God and in a manner see God when He chooses.

DOHNANYI
I would be happy just to see an end to Hitler and his gang.

DIETRICH
May God so bless us.

THE MOURNING DOVE COOS AGAIN.
LIGHTS DOWN ON THE SET.
DIETRICH AND DOHNANYI EXIT.
AS THE STAGEHANDS PREPARE THE
NEXT SCENE, THE MUSIC OF AN
ORGAN-GRINDER IS HEARD.

SCENE 1D

SETTING:

WE ARE IN A BERLIN PARK IN EARLY NOVEMBER 1942. AT LEAST TWO PARK BENCHES ABUT THE BACKSTAGE EDGE OF TIER 1. OTHER PARK FIXTURES, SUCH AS A LAMPPOST AND TRASH RECEPTACLE, AND SUGGESTIONS OF VEGETATION MAY FESTOON THE SET AD LIBITUM. THE WEATHER IS OVERCAST BUT NOT RAINY.

AT RISE:

AS THE LIGHTS COME UP ON THE SET, THE NOISES OF THE ORGAN GRINDER AND CHILDREN TAPER OFF. JUST BEFORE DIETRICH AND EBERHARD ENTER THE SCENE, A BOY AND GIRL (EXTRAS) MAY RUN ACROSS THE STAGE IN A GAME OF CHASE. DIETRICH AND MOTHER ENTER FROM OPPOSITE SIDES OF THE STAGE, JOINING EACH OTHER AT A PARK BENCH, WHERE THEY SIT DOWN.

DIETRICH
I saw you watching the Punch and Judy show.

MOTHER
It was delightful. Brings back memories.

DIETRICH
(AS A SIGNAL)
They've been going on for hundreds of years.

DIETRICH AND MOTHER LOOK ABOUT.

MOTHER
Thanks for agreeing to meet me here. I know this must seem highly unusual.

DIETRICH
It is. But I could tell when we talked you were concerned.

MOTHER
One must be careful what one says on the phone. We're sure that it's tapped.

DIETRICH
I gather you don't want me coming to the house.

MOTHER
I want you to know your father and I are certain the house is being watched, almost constantly. It's gotten to be some-what nerve-wracking for all of us, especially Klaus.

DIETRICH
Does Klaus think the house is being watched because of my activities?

MOTHER

He hasn't said so. But he suggested the next time you were in Berlin you should meet with either Father or me somewhere other than the house for starters.

DIETRICH

None of us wants you in harm's way. I don't know why they're watching you. Why didn't Father come?

MOTHER

I said I wanted to meet you alone. I'm the one that asks the questions Father won't ask. How goes the therapeutic effort?

DIETRICH

Truly, I've no idea. Hans is in a better position to tell you.

MOTHER

Whenever we see him now it's too public to ask.

DIETRICH

I didn't think you would want to know.

MOTHER

That's Father's position, not mine.

DIETRICH

Yes, well, I'm very much on the periphery of this whole thing. Anyway, from what Hans says, it may be more than a year before anything happens, if you know what I mean.

MOTHER

By then other powers may have swept over Germany. I think you entered into this effort as a practical way of helping people—really the only practical way of helping large numbers. Perhaps you should refocus your efforts on helping a few people get out. We've got enough other people in the family—Hans, Klaus, Rudiger—working on the therapeutic effort. Your father and I can provide some money to help you with additional exit activities.

DIETRICH
Thank you, but getting people out has proven more difficult than I would have imagined. In an Abwehr operation called "U7" we managed to get only a very few people out. I can't get many out if everything has to be done by the book.

MOTHER
What book?

DIETRICH
The book of regulations. Those people we got out in U7 left under the guise they'd be Abwehr agents in Switzerland. I've probably said too much.

MOTHER
I'm your mother. Go on...about this U7.

DIETRICH
Admiral Canaris had to personally ask Himmler to let these Jewish people out as agents.

MOTHER
I see. A blessing from the SS swamp was considered better than a secret removal of these people from German soil.

DIETRICH
Exactly...but that is one of the constraints of the Abwehr. After all, it's an arm of the government.

MOTHER

Canaris must be a Prussian—everything by the book.

DIETRICH

You shouldn't be so hard on the Prussians. I sometimes think the staunchest opponents to the Modernists are Prussian. Anyway, I'm developing a relation with a Prussian. I've been wanting to tell you and Father.

MOTHER

I'd heard something. That's another reason I wanted to see you alone.

ULRICH ENTERS DRESSED
IN A SUIT AND OVERCOAT.

DIETRICH

Forgive me for not speaking sooner.

DIETRICH NOTICES ULRICH.

ULRICH

Bonhoeffer?

DIETRICH STANDS.

DIETRICH
(EXTENDING HIS HAND)

My dear Schmidt! What a surprise. Greetings. May I introduce my mother?

ULRICH
(NODDING BUT KEEPING HIS HANDS TO HIMSELF)
Pastor, Madam, good day to you.

MOTHER
Good day, Mr...

ULRICH
Schmidt.

DIETRICH
How is your wife and child? Was it a boy or a girl?

ULRICH
In my family things are well. I'm expecting a transfer soon out of Berlin.

DIETRICH
I hope you will be transferred to a healthy new location.

ULRICH
As you yourself taught, we can't be selfish. I will serve wherever I'm sent. If you'll excuse me, Madam Bonhoeffer.

DIETRICH
Please accept my best wishes for your wife and child.

ULRICH
(SALUTING)
Hail Hitler!

MOTHER STANDS.
DIETRICH AND MOTHER SALUTE.

DIETRICH AND MOTHER
Hail Hitler.

ULRICH EXITS.

MOTHER

You shouldn't stay in Berlin, Dietrich. I can't see that you should be participating in this replacement therapy when your first duty is to the church. How can you forget Christ's warning to Peter that those who live by the sword must die by the sword?

DIETRICH

I won't try to soften one word of our Lord. But how can we love our neighbor as ourselves and not live by the sword in modern Germany? Even higher than my duty as a pastor is my duty to Christ.

MOTHER

Yes, yet it is written, "Let every person be subject to the governing authorities. For there is no authority except from God, and those that exist have been instituted by God."

DIETRICH

St Paul wrote that. But in his letter to the Romans he went on... "For rulers are not a terror to good conduct, but to bad." Our so-called rulers don't fit St Paul's definition. Anyway, St Paul's admonition cannot be decisive when placed against Christ's admonition to love our neighbors. When others are robbed of the gift of life, I can't idly stand by, especially when I've been given an opportunity to act.

MOTHER

So I expected you'd argue. You are my son and I'm proud of you. Just don't act foolishly.

DIETRICH

Only as a fool for Christ.

(PAUSE)

I wonder if Ulrich will report us being here.

MOTHER

He may have been following you.

DIETRICH

I don't think so. He seemed surprised to see me.

MOTHER

He may be a good actor. Who is the woman you alluded to? When will Father and I meet her?

DIETRICH

When she can travel from Prussia to Berlin. Her name is Maria von Wedemeyer.

MOTHER

You've talked of the Wedemeyers before. Mrs Wedemeyer is a strong supporter of the Confessing Church, as I recall.

DIETRICH

Yes.

MOTHER

How long have you known the daughter? This Maria is a daughter, isn't she?

DIETRICH

She is. Not very long.

MOTHER

Does she know you're living on the edge—so far as the world is concerned?

DIETRICH

Yes.

MOTHER

And you intend to marry her?

DIETRICH

Very much so.

MOTHER

Does Mr Wedemeyer approve? Have you asked?

DIETRICH

Mrs Wedemeyer's husband—and son—were recently killed on the Eastern Front.

MOTHER

There's lots of that these days. I would imagine Mrs Wedemeyer would have mixed feelings about allowing her daughter to marry. She'd want her around as a consolation even while wanting her to start a new family, of her own. That I can understand.

DIETRICH

Actually, I think she would be opposed to a marriage, at least right now. I don't know how long Maria and I want to delay my asking permission.

MOTHER

What does that mean—that Mrs Wedemeyer would be opposed?

DIETRICH

Maria is only 18.

MOTHER

I see.

DIETRICH

She is mature and wise beyond her years.

MOTHER

I guess if you live a barely possible existence God might grant you a barely possible wife.

DIETRICH CASTS UP HIS HANDS,
SMILES, AND LAUGHS. LIGHTS DOWN
AS SOUNDS OF THE ORGAN GRINDER
AND CHILDREN ARE HEARD ONCE
AGAIN, BEFORE FADING OUT. DIETRICH
AND MOTHER EXIT. TRAIN STATION
NOISES ARE HEARD AS THE
STAGEHANDS PREPARE THE NEXT SCENE.

SCENE 1E

SETTING:

WE ARE IN AT AN OPEN-AIR STATION CAFÉ IN BERLIN, FEBRUARY 1943. WHISTLES AND STATION ANNOUNCEMENTS ARE HEARD IN THE BACKGROUND AND PERHAPS EVEN A MILITARY BAND.

AT RISE:

AS THE LIGHTS COME UP ON THE SET, THE STATION NOISES ARE SOFTENED. KLAUS AND CHRISTINE ARE SEATED AT A TABLE. KARL-FREDERICH JOINS THEM, SETTING HIS ATTACHE ON THE FLOOR NEXT TO HIS SEAT. EVERYONE IS WEARING AN OVERCOAT.

KARL-FREDERICH
Christine, Klaus—greetings!

CHRISTINE AND KLAUS
GREET KARL-FREDERICH WARMLY.

CHRISTINE

I'm glad we could get together this afternoon on your way back to Leipzig.

KARL-FREDERICH

No problem. Where's Dietrich?

CHRISTINE

He couldn't come.

KLAUS

No surprise.

KARL-FREDERICH

Is he even in Berlin?

KLAUS

He flits around a lot. Who knows? He may even be in Italy.

KARL-FREDERICH

Why Italy?

CHRISTINE

He's doing something for the Vatican.

KLAUS

Enough said on that subject. I'm sure Dietrich is greatly exulted in this work. It feeds his sense of self-importance.

CHRISTINE

You've never been able to accept our brother's religious commitment.

KLAUS

It has always seemed to me deeply childish...when what we need are grounded men and women. If the development of the nation is ever to take place, we need mature people all the way around, not people with pieties foaming from their mouth.

CHRISTINE

I don't think the pieties foam from his mouth. They gush up from his heart—and I for one, no, I for two, for I speak for Hans, too, know we are far wiser and far braver than we'd otherwise be if it weren't for Dietrich and his like.

KLAUS
(LOOKING AT KARL-FREDERICH)

What do you think?

KARL-FREDERICH

I think we had better keep our conversation pretty short, not least because I have the Leipzig train to catch.

KLAUS

Don't evade.

KARL-FREDERICH

I've always been agnostic on religious matters, as you well know. I remind you our brother returned to Germany from the States in the summer of 1939. He could have stayed at Columbia University and been a center of attention, if he'd wanted to be. Instead he chose to come back, facing all that we know now and he expected then.

KLAUS

You make it sound like he's a hero. You came back on the same ship and have never acted like a hero.

CHRISTINE

I wouldn't say Dietrich acts like a hero. On the contrary, he very much wants a "normal life," as he calls it.

KARL-FREDERICH

I came back from Chicago because I didn't want to be separated from family. We all could see the war coming.

KLAUS

There you have it. At least you're capable of self-insight and an honesty about what you find.

KARL-FREDERICH

You are being harsh on Dietrich. Anyway for him it wasn't family that brought him back.

KLAUS

Oh, come-on.

KARL-FREDERICH

Oh, he's never pretended his family and friends are unimportant. He cherishes all of us, even you, Klaus.

CHRISTINE

What is it about you two?

KLAUS

You mean Dietrich and me?

CHRISTINE

Yes.

KLAUS

He's always been so self-important.

KARL-FREDERICH
I hadn't noticed.

KLAUS
You're so busy being the scientist.

CHRISTINE
Our brother is merely earnest...as are you, Klaus.

KARL-FREDERICH
(LAUGHING)
How about me?

CHRISTINE
You, too, there's plenty to go around in the family.

KLAUS
Maybe so. But for all his forth-rightness, Dietrich can be too clever by half.

CHRISTINE
You have different operating styles.

KLAUS
His are either dangerous or hilarious.

KARL-FREDERICH
Given where we're at, describe a hilarity, but keep it short. I've a train to catch.

CHRISTINE
We're supposed to be discussing Father's birthday party. And I want to get your signatures for the book we bought for Papa.

KARL-FREDERICH

You found it?

CHRISTINE

Yes.

KLAUS

Good for you.

KARL-FREDERICH
(TAKING OUT A PEN)

Here. I'll sign it right now.

CHRISTINE
(HANDING A BOOK TO KARL-FREDERICH)

Sign it up front. Add a sentiment, too.

KARL-FREDERICH WRITES
IN THE BOOK AS KLAUS SPEAKS.

KLAUS
(TAKING OUT A PEN)

Are you still interested in the hilarious?

KARL-FREDERICH
(STILL WRITING)

We can always use a laugh.

KLAUS

I was going to tell you anyway, but this fits in with the category. Dietrich is planning on getting married.

KARL-FREDERICH

That is neither hilarious nor news. That's normal and old business. Is he finally linking up with that lady...?

CHRISTINE

She's long gone. No it's someone else. Dietrich told me about her recently but asked me not to mention it to anyone outside the family. I told Klaus...but hadn't gotten around to telling you.

KARL-FREDERICH
(HANDING THE BOOK TO KLAUS)

Oh, I'm not offended. Who's the lady?

KLAUS

You mean, Who's the girl?

KARL-FREDERICH

What's her name?

CHRISTINE

Maria von Wedemeyer.

KLAUS

She's 18 years old.

KARL-FREDERICH

I can see why Dietrich would want to, shall we say, cover the news.

KLAUS

Why did he decide to marry a girl of 18 years of age?

KARL-FREDERICH

From her perspective or his?

KLAUS
Now that you ask it, from hers.

KARL-FREDERICH
We're at war. Look at any German town or city and you'll find very few available, marriageable men. Our brother Dietrich is an aberration.

KLAUS
In more ways than one.

CHRISTINE
Don't be so hard on him. You know he'll be devoted and loyal to whomever he marries. Can anyone ask for more?

KLAUS
Money helps, as you well know. She could marry a man with a real job.

CHRISTINE
Like yours?

KLAUS
(KLAUS HANDS THE BOOK TO CHRISTINE)
Lufthansa pays real money. Dietrich survives on hand-outs. How can he possibly support a wife?

KARL-FREDERICH
Our dear brother would say the Lord provides.

KLAUS
But not forever.

CHRISTINE
Not in this life, but so far…

KARL-FREDERICH
Our brother survives.

KLAUS
I notice Dietrich hasn't signed the book.

KARL-FREDERICH
Nor has Sabine, but of course that's impossible.

CHRISTINE
Perhaps someday we can travel to Oxford to see Sabine and Leibholz. I miss not being able to travel.

KLAUS
If a war were to go away that might be possible once again.

CHRISTINE
Klaus, you're always complaining that Dietrich is careless.

KLAUS
It's noisy in here. And unlike Dietrich...well, enough.

KARL-FREDERICH
I wonder what the weather is like in Oxford today. It seems so far away.

CHRISTINE
Not as far as the distance between two brothers.

KLAUS
Let's complete the party arrangements. Karl-Frederich must catch his train.

KARL-FREDERICH
Indeed.

LIGHTS DOWN ON THE SET. CHRISTINE,
KLAUS, AND KARL-FREDERICH EXIT.
A PIANO PLAYING SCHUBERT
LIEDER IS NOW HEARD,
AS THE NEXT SCENE IS PREPARED.

SCENE 1F

SETTING:

WE ARE AT THE ENTRY HALL OF THE BONHOEFFER RESIDENCE IN BERLIN, 31 MARCH 1943. TIER 1 IS THE FOYER OF THE ENTRY HALL, WITH THE STREET ENTRANCE ON STAGE RIGHT. STAGE LEFT AFFORDS ENTRY INTO THE PARLOR, WHERE A LARGE BROOD OF FAMILY AND FRIENDS ARE GATHERED, HERE AT THE BONHOEFFER HOUSEHOLD FOR THE CELE-BRATION OF FATHER'S 75TH BIRTHDAY. THE PRODUCTION MAY—BUT NEED NOT—LAV-ISH THE STAGE SPACE WITH ENTRYWAY ACCOUTERMENTS: SIDE TABLES, A CHAN-DELIER, PERHAPS EVEN A BACKDROP DEPICTING A WALL EMBELLISHED WITH PAINTINGS. TIER 2 SHOULD BE OBSCURED BY THIS BACKDROP OR LEFT DARKENED. ALL ENTRIES AND EXITS IN THIS SCENE WILL BE ON TIER 1. ANYONE APPEARING IN THIS SCENE SHOULD BE DRESSED TO THE NINES.

AT RISE:

AS THE LIGHTS COME UP ON THE SET,

VOICES ARE HEARD COMING FROM OFF-STAGE LEFT, AS WELL AS THE PIANO PLAYING OF A SCHUBERT SONG. FATHER, DIETRICH, KLAUS, AND KARL-FREDERICH SAUNTER IN, TALKING, FROM STAGE LEFT (FROM THE PARLOR). LED BY FATHER THEY WALK DOWN TO THE STAGE LEVEL. ALL HAVE DRINKS IN HAND.

FATHER

I can't tell you how happy your mother and I are to have you all under our roof at the same time—well, almost all. Sabine, of course, can't be here. But we all know she and dear Leibholz couldn't have survived if they were still here. So, we are very fortunate.

KARL-FREDERICH

We're happy so many of us could be here on your 75th birthday celebration, Papa.

MOTHER ENTERS FROM STAGE LEFT.

MOTHER

Aren't you going to join the rest of us?

FATHER

In a minute, Mama.

MOTHER EXITS.

FATHER

I want to drink a toast in here that we can't drink in there.

KLAUS
(ALARMED)

I hope...

FATHER

It's merely a toast to your extracurricular, therapeutic activities.

KARL-FREDERICH

To all such extracurricular activities, if I may amend that, Dad.

KLAUS

We shouldn't even be thinking about any of that; we must be discreet. Think of the help around here today. It's the careless discussion that can lead to disaster.

KARL-FREDERICH

But this is not open, Klaus.

KLAUS

Open enough. It's the least indiscretion that could destroy the efforts now underway.

FATHER

Klaus, don't trouble yourself. I know very little and your mother and I intend to keep it that way.

DIETRICH

Maybe we should get around to the toast.

KLAUS

If we must, shouldn't we have a few others in here, too. Hans, for one, is right in the next room. He's very much a key man in the extracurricular activities. In fairness, let me go get...

FATHER

This is enough...

DIETRICH

Perhaps I should get Chris.

KLAUS

I already suggested as much.

FATHER

Yes, we should have Christine in here, too. But quickly, if you know what I mean. Quickly, Dietrich, go ahead...

DIETRICH

Yes.

DIETRICH EXITS.

KLAUS

Really, we must be careful, Father.

FATHER

You're right. But I turn 75 only once.

DIETRICH ENTERS WITH CHRISTINE. SHE DOESN'T HAVE A GLASS.

KLAUS
Look! She can't drink a toast. She doesn't have a drink.

KARL-FREDERICH
Always the lawyer, Klaus.

CHRISTINE
(TAKING DIETRICH'S GLASS)
I'll be sharing with Dietrich, Papa.

FATHER
Good. To my children. From one therapist to other therapists. Here's to your extracurricular activities.

KARL-FREDERICH, CHRISTINE, AND
FINALLY KLAUS RAISE THEIR GLASSES,
LIKE FATHER, AND OFFER "PROSIT'S"
BEFORE PARTAKING OF THEIR DRINKS.
MOTHER ENTERS. CHRISTINE RETURNS
DIETRICH'S GLASS TO DIETRICH.
HE TAKES A SIP FROM IT.

MOTHER
Come on, if you will, Papa, boys, Christine.

DOORBELL RINGS.

MOTHER
Who could that be? We're all here.

FATHER
Where's the maid?

                         MOTHER
I'll get the door.

           MOTHER WALKS TO STAGE RIGHT AND
           OPENS THE "STREET DOOR", WHICH MAY
           BE OUT OF SIGHT. CHANCLRY REP AND
           CHANCLRY ESCORT ENTER WALKING TO
           CENTER TIER 1, FOLLOWED BY MOTHER.
           THE CHANCLRY REP SPOTS FATHER.

                      CHANCLRY REP
                       (SALUTING)
Hail victory!

                         FATHER
                       (SALUTING)
Hail victory!

                          ALL
                       (SALUTING)
Hail victory!

           THE SOUND OF THE PIANO STOPS. ANY
           NOISE HERETOFORE COMING FROM THE
           PARLOR, OFFSTAGE, IS NOW HUSHED.
           FATHER WALKS UP TO TIER 1.

                      CHANCLRY REP
                  (EXTENDING HIS HAND)
Doctor Bonhoeffer, I am Colonel Wallenstein, sent from
the Chancellery by our Leader. It is a pleasure to meet you.

FATHER
(SHAKING HANDS)
Indeed. Indeed. What is the occasion, sir?

CHANCLRY REP
(AMUSED)
You should ask? It's your 75th birthday. I am pleased to announce the Leader has bestowed upon you the Goethe Award, annually given to that German who is recognized as having made a lifetime of contributions to German culture.

FATHER
I am stunned. I'm deeply moved.

WITH A NOD FROM THE CHANCLRY REP THE CHANCLRY ESCORT COMES FORWARD WITH A BOX IN HAND, STOPS, CLICKS HIS HEELS, AND OPENS THE BOX. FROM THE BOX THE CHANCLRY REP LIFTS A MEDALLION ON A RIBBON.

CHANCLRY REP
All Germany hails you.

FATHER LOWERS HIS NECK AS THE CHANCLRY REP PLACES THE GOETHE MEDALLION AROUND FATHER'S NECK.

FATHER
Thank you.

                    CHANCLRY REP
                    (SALUTING)
Hail Hitler!

                        ALL
                    (SALUTING)
Hail Hitler!

                    CHANCLRY REP
                    (SALUTING)
Hail Victory!

                        ALL
                    (SALUTING)
Hail Victory!

                      (PAUSE)

                      MOTHER
Would you care to join us?

                    CHANCLRY REP
Thank you. That is most kind of you to offer but we must return to the Chancellery. Anyway it looks like you have a full house.

                 CHANCLRY REP SHAKES
              MOTHER'S HAND, THEN SHAKES
                 FATHER'S HAND AGAIN.

                    CHANCLRY REP
Congratulations! Good day.

(SALUTING)

Hail Hitler!

ALL
(SALUTING)

Hail Hitler!

CHANCLRY REP AND CHANCLRY
ESCORT EXIT STAGE RIGHT,
FOLLOWED BY MOTHER, WHO
RETURNS TO FATHER, ONCE SHE HAS
SEEN THE CHANCELLERY PEOPLE OFF.
FATHER IS FONDLING THE MEDALLION.

FATHER

I'm stunned. Why would Hitler have bestowed this on me?

KARL-FREDERICH

You were Germany's first psychiatrist. You are her leading psychiatrist. Why else?

FATHER

But I've contributed nothing to the war effort.

KLAUS

To be sure. But you've written a number of articles over the years attacking Sigmund Freud's ideas.

FATHER

That's because Freud's ideas are a swamp.

KARL-FREDERICH

Klaus is not suggesting your criticisms aren't well directed.

KLAUS

No, the criticism has been deserved. But because Freud was Jewish you endeared yourself to the Party.

MOTHER

Anything your father had to say about Freud was directed at his ideas.

KARL-FREDERICH

Of course.

DIETRICH

We all know that. Your colleagues know that, too.

KLAUS

But the question of the hour is this, how will the Party use this award?

DIETRICH

We can't worry about that because there's nothing we can do about it anyway. We must count the award as a blessing.

THE MUTED PLAYING OF
A WALTZ IS HEARD.

KLAUS

Ever thus your view!

DIETRICH

But it is. Given that the Leader himself has chosen to give Father this award, his minions will exercise care in anything having to do with Father—and with Mother. I shall thank God that Father has been given this award.

MOTHER

Yes, we must give Him thanks. But let's not talk with dread. We must never be brave by half measures. We, Father and I, are proud of our boys, your wives, our girls, and your husbands. Now let's go in and join the celebration we've prepared for you, Papa.

FATHER KISSES MOTHER
AFFECTIONATELY. THE
OTHERS APPLAUD.

FATHER

Let's go, Christine, boys.

FATHER, MOTHER, CHRISTINE
AND KARL-FREDERICH EXIT.

DIETRICH

It's really too bad that Sabine and Leibholz weren't able to be here.

KLAUS

You're not really suggesting they should have been here.

DIETRICH

Of course not. Leibholz couldn't have been here in any event—he would have been carried off by the Gestapo.

KLAUS

Then it really makes little sense to mourn his absence. Let's be clearheaded, my dear brother. You're always advising that to others. Maybe it's about time you abided by your own recipes for success.

DIETRICH

I can't say I offer any recipes for success.

KLAUS

Isn't that the truth and what do you offer as a man? Who the devil do you think you are anyway?

DIETRICH

What do you mean? This conversation is taking a turn that suggests we should have it at another time.

KLAUS

When we get to the heart of the matter you're more than happy to take flight. Well, I'll keep it short. You seem to think you're some sort of angel in disguise at the Abwehr. Maybe that's an occupational hazard in Army Intelligence. But I think it says something about you.

DIETRICH

What does it say?

KLAUS

You are happy enough to play at life, to advise others how to slog along. But you yourself are detached from all the horrors below you, the horror inflicted on Europe and Germany. You are above it all, in the end and in the beginning. So you do foolish things, imperiling the therapeutic effort that's underway.

DIETRICH

How so?

KLAUS

For one thing, running a courier service between Germany and the Vatican is a foolish thing. What can the

Vatican do to effect change here, for God's sake?

CHRISTINE ENTERS.

CHRISTINE
Mama wants you in here. Come on.

DIETRICH
We're coming. The Vatican, too, is a part of the struggle.

KLAUS
You have a much different perspective than I. We've got to be practical. But even when you're more practical you're dangerous to the cause.

DIETRICH
How?

KLAUS
We all agree the persecution of peoples is unacceptable. But how could you have persuaded the Abwehr to put Jewish families in Switzerland under the guise they were spies?

CHRISTINE (FIRMLY)
Klaus! Hold your tongue. Come on in here, both of you.

DIETRICH
I was told there was no other way the Abwehr could participate in extricating them from Germany.

KLAUS
Sending them into Switzerland as spies required the approval of Himmler himself.

DIETRICH

As for myself I would prefer not to deal with that man or his gang. But I cannot imperil the Abwehr's...

KLAUS

So you, too, compromise.

DIETRICH

If you have a better way of getting marked people out of harm's way, let me know. We both know the best way is "therapy," as we're calling it.

KLAUS

Precisely. Precisely. That's precisely why you shouldn't be initiating these fool's errands, where only angels and fools rush in. They only attract the authorities. Be a man, be clear-headed, stop imperiling the project, and stop putting us in harm's way.

DIETRICH

Forgive me...

KLAUS

I don't want to hear any of this forgive business. Just be a man.

KLAUS EXITS IN HASTE. DIETRICH
LOOKS AT CHRISTINE, WHO SMILES AND
BECKONS HIM. DIETRICH AND CHRISTINE
EXIT AS THE LIGHTS GO OUT. WHILE THE
STAGEHANDS PREPARE THE SET FOR THE
NEXT SCENE THE SOUNDS FROM
THE PARTY TAPER OFF. A PHONOGRAPH
RECORDING OF "HE'S GOT THE WHOLE

WORLD IN HIS HANDS" BEGINS, TIMED
TO END IN THE FOLLOWING SCENE,
JUST AS DIETRICH ENTERS.

SCENE 1G

SETTING:

WE ARE IN THE BONHOEFFER RESIDENCE IN BERLIN ON 5 APRIL 1943. A PHONOGRAPH PLAYER RESTS ON THE DOWN STAGE EDGE OF TIER 1. THERE IS A TELEPHONE ON A TABLE. EXCEPT FOR THESE FURNISHINGS THE REMAINDER OF THE SET SHOULD BE KEPT DARKENED.

AT RISE:

AS THE LIGHTS COME UP ON THE SET, EBERHARD IS SEEN LISTENING TO THE LAST ROUND OF "HE'S GOT THE WHOLE WORLD IN HIS HANDS."

DIETRICH ENTERS WITH AN OPENED
BOTTLE OF WINE AND TWO GLASSES.
DURING THE FOLLOWING DIETRICH
SETS THE GLASSES ON THE TABLE,
POURS DRINKS, AND HANDS
A GLASS TO EBERHARD.

EBERHARD
I think that's one of my favorite spirituals.

DIETRICH
It's beautiful, isn't it?

EBERHARD
I'm glad you introduced them to us at the seminary. They are such a comfort.

DIETRICH
They are. So when do you expect to suit up for the Army?

EBERHARD
They didn't say. They told me I should be prepared to leave on three days' notice.

DIETRICH
I'm going to miss you. I'm viewing this selfishly, but not just selfishly. I fear what will happen to you.

EBERHARD
There's nothing we can do.

DIETRICH
Maybe there is. I should call Hans.

EBERHARD
What can he do?

DIETRICH
I don't know. Maybe he'll have an idea.

DIETRICH RAISES HIS GLASS. SO DOES
EBERHARD. THE TWO SAY "PROSIT,"
AT FIRST SIP, THEN DRINK A BIT MORE
BEFORE SETTING THEIR GLASSES DOWN.

EBERHARD

I don't want any special treatment. Let God's hand show.

DIETRICH

God gets very little opportunity to show His hand in the German army these days since even the most elementary decencies have been supplanted by the "superior" norms of Modernist man.

EBERHARD

God won't place any burden on me that with His help I can't handle.

DIETRICH
(DIALING THE TELEPHONE)

God be praised, but let me call Hans.

EBERHARD

Please, just to share the news, not to ask for special treatment or anything like that.

DIETRICH

Hans might be the very help our Lord wants you to have. I should have thought of this before.

EBERHARD

We'd agreed some time ago there was nothing we should do.

DIETRICH

That was then and this is now. It's taking the longest time for anyone to answer...Oh, hello.

DIETRICH COVERS THE SPEAKER END OF THE PHONE HANDSET, GENTLY PLACING THE HANDSET ON THE CRADLE OF THE PHONE.

EBERHARD

What's wrong?

DIETRICH

A stranger answered the phone at Hans and Christine's.

EBERHARD

Yes?

DIETRICH

It must be the Gestapo. Hans has been arrested and they're ransacking the house for evidence.

EBERHARD

You don't know that.

DIETRICH

I have this feeling I'm next on the arrest list. Do me the favor of getting word to Maria.

EBERHARD

If you think that's what happened, of course. But how do you know?

DIETRICH

I know.

(BRIEF PAUSE)

It's been almost a week since the birthday party and I still haven't introduced her to Mama and Papa. I had hoped...

EBERHARD

Look, don't worry about that. I'll introduce her when she's able to get to Berlin.

DIETRICH

Good, good. That would be most kind.

(BRIEF PAUSE)

I must go up to my room to arrange things to *help* the Gestapo find certain papers.

EBERHARD

You'd better get a big meal down before they come.

DIETRICH

Good idea. Will you go tell my parents?

EBERHARD

I will. When the Gestapo comes, play the simpleton pastor.

DIETRICH

I barely have the wisdom of a simpleton, but I must learn to be a serpent, alas.

EBERHARD

You can say you were merely following orders, like a good German.

DIETRICH AND EBERHARD LAUGH THEN EMBRACE EACH OTHER IN A HUG.

EBERHARD
(AS HE AND DIETRICH DISENGAGE
FROM THE HUG)

Rely on God's protection.

DIETRICH

It may not be God's will that I be protected now.

EBERHARD

You don't believe that.

DIETRICH

I do. There's a time to act for Christ and a time to suffer with Christ.

EBERHARD

I think you've acted for Christ.

DIETRICH

Some would say rather foolishly, but I thank you.

(PAUSE)

I believe I have been no less Christian in aiding the plot to overthrow these murderers than in teaching seminary students. That's a terrible thing to say, perhaps, but these are terrifying times. Pray for me, Eberhard. Pray for my parents and for Maria. Help them to the extent that you can. I know you will.

EBERHARD

I will by God's grace. I'll go get your mother so they can put together a meal.

DIETRICH

Yes, do. Thank you.

LIGHTS DOWN ON THE STAGE SET.

CURTAIN DOWN.

END OF ACT 1

BONHOEFFER: Act 2

Boldface characters listed below appear in both acts, plain-text characters in Act 1 only, and *italicized* in Act 2 only.

	ACT 2 SCENE:	A	B	C	D	E	F	G	H	I	J	K	L	M
1	**Dietrich**	A	B	C	D	E	F	G	H	I	J	K	L	M
2	**Eberhard**				D	E								
2	*Camp Guard 1*											K	L	M
3	**Ulrich**	A										K	L	
3	Chanclry Escort													
3	*Tegel Guard 1*		B	C			F							
3	*Tegel Guard 2**								H					
4	**Karl-Frederich**													
4	Eden													
4	*Uncle Paul*							G						
4	*RHSO Guard*									I	J			
4	*Camp Guard 2*											K	L	M
5	**Klaus**										J			
5	Dohnanyi													
5	*Sonderkothen*			C		E			H					M
6	**Father**													
6	Churchill													
6	*Canaris*									I		K		M
6	*Tegel Sergeant*						F	G						
7	**Mother**				D									
7	Secretary 1													
7	Patron F													
7	*Camp Guard 3*												L	M
8	**Christine**													
8	Lady													
8	*Camp Guard 4*													M
9	*Maria*		B		D		F							
9	Secretary 2													
9	Waitress													
10	*Rechter*	A		C		E	F	G						
10	Chanclry Rep													
10	Patron M													

106

SCENE 2A

SETTING:

WE ARE AT AN AIRLESS HOLDING CELL IN TEGEL MILITARY INTERROGATION PRISON, BERLIN, 17 APRIL 1943, 12 DAYS AFTER DIETRICH'S ARREST. THE SET IS DARK EXCEPT FOR THE LIGHTING ON DIETRICH.

AT RISE:

DIETRICH IS HUDDLED ON THE STAGE LEVEL. HE IS LEANING AGAINST A WALL WHERE TIER 1 RISES ABOVE THE STAGE LEVEL. HE IS IN DISHEVELED VERSIONS OF THE CLOTHES HE WORE AT THE CONCLUSION OF ACT 1. HE DOES NOT APPEAR DISTRAUGHT. WITH INCREASING NOISE, THREE METAL DOORS ARE SUCCESSIVELY HEARD CLANGING OPEN. RECHTER ENTERS ON TIER 1 FOLLOWED BY ULRICH, IN TRENCH COAT AND HAT. RECHTER AND ULRICH WALK DOWN STEPS TO THE STAGE LEVEL. RECHTER "OPENS" THE "DOOR" TO DIETRICH'S CELL. RECHTER ENTERS THE CELL FIRST.

RECHTER

Prisoner Bonhoeffer! Attention!

DIETRICH STANDS AT ATTENTION.
ULRICH ENTERS THE CELL.

ULRICH

Corporal, dismissed.

RECHTER

Yes sir.

RECHTER EXITS CELL AND STAGE.

ULRICH

Do you recognize me?

DIETRICH

It would help if there were more light in here.

ULRICH

Where you're going the light will be better.

DIETRICH

Where is that?

ULRICH

Up. How long have you been in Tegel?

DIETRICH

This is the twelfth day, if my reckoning is correct, sir.

ULRICH

It is. Biblical isn't it?

DIETRICH

Ulrich Schmidt!

ULRICH

You needn't be familiar with me.

DIETRICH

In a way I'm not surprised we should be meeting here. Have you assisted in my case?

ULRICH

You shouldn't be familiar with me.

DIETRICH

As you wish. Permission to make inquiries, sir.

ULRICH

Granted. Keep them short. They'll be coming soon to move you.

DIETRICH

Where, sir?

ULRICH

To another cell, more suited to your family connections.

DIETRICH

Family connections?

ULRICH

The Army authorities have just tumbled to the fact your maternal uncle is military commandant of Berlin. They have no interest in aggravating him, especially since you were arrested by the Gestapo. Like so many Army types they have a contempt for the Gestapo.

DIETRICH

You mean I'm to be given preferential treatment because of my family connection?

ULRICH

Precisely.

DIETRICH

That is contemptible.

ULRICH

But you'll take it.

DIETRICH

I know it could be far worse than I've gotten so far.

ULRICH

Have they exercised you?

DIETRICH

No.

ULRICH

I mean beaten you.

DIETRICH

Not yet. Just verbal abuse, which is beyond decency, of course. I could use a good meal, too.

ULRICH

Well, now you'll have the luxury treatment, such as it is: a cell with a bed, a light, even a small window. You'll be able to get books. You might be able to watch history pass you by.

DIETRICH

I'd rather be in it.

ULRICH

You'll be able to write your fiancée or parents every other week. Eventually they may be able to visit you.

DIETRICH

Do I have you to thank for that?

ULRICH

No. These are simply the regulations that prevail where you'll be held. The Army is bound up in old-fashioned notions of chivalry.

DIETRICH

Thank God for the Army.

ULRICH

From an old pacifist, no less.

DIETRICH

I've never been a pacifist, just a Christian.

ULRICH

You never taught me the difference.

DIETRICH

There's much I didn't teach you, it seems, but it's not my job to give you a passing or failing grade in life.

ULRICH

Thank you, but no detours, please, into theology.

DIETRICH

Why have you come, if I may ask?...sir.

ULRICH

I'm here to tell you not to be lulled by Army hospitality. You are here because of the Gestapo. If you want out, cooperation is the key.

DIETRICH

"Cooperation." That can be a code word for many things.

ULRICH

For instance?

DIETRICH

For moral indifference.

ULRICH

The Gestapo doesn't delude itself with the thought you can be persuaded into indifference.

DIETRICH

Then it would appear there is little reason for them to talk with me or me with them.

ULRICH

On the contrary. The Gestapo is looking for disclosure.

DIETRICH

I've nothing to disclose.

ULRICH

I'm sure.

DIETRICH

You can be sure. But thank you for warning me. Your consideration is more to your favor than your occupation.

ULRICH

Watch what you say.

DIETRICH

It's hard for me to forget who you are supposed to be...sir.

ULRICH

I detect another whiff of theology.

DIETRICH

Then let's stay away from theology. How about your family?

ULRICH

I've been here long enough.

DIETRICH

Don't go. What about the boy, the girl?

ULRICH

The child was defective—a cleft lip. The Party doesn't want recidivism. Keep that in mind, Prisoner Bonhoeffer.

ULRICH EXITS THE CELL AND THE STAGE SET. RECHTER ENTERS THE STAGE.

DIETRICH

May God forgive us.

RECHTER ARRIVES AT DIETRICH'S CELL.

RECHTER

Pastor Bonhoeffer, may I get you a cup of water?

DIETRICH

Thank you. That would be most kind, Corporal.

LIGHTS DOWN ON THE STAGE SET.
RECHTER EXITS.

SCENE 2B

<u>SETTING</u>:

WE ARE AT THE VISITING ROOM IN TEGEL PRISON IN EARLY SUMMER 1943. TWO BENCHES FACE ONE ANOTHER ON THE STAGE LEVEL, SEPARATED BY A CORDON OR SMALL BARRICADE. THROUGHOUT THE SCENE TIER 1 IS LARGELY DARK AND TIER 2 IS KEPT DARK OR OBSCURED.

<u>AT RISE</u>:

AS THE LIGHTS COME UP ON THE STAGE LEVEL AND TIER 1 LEVEL, TEGEL GUARD 1, AT STAGE LEVEL, IS SEEN CASUALLY PACING BACK AND FORTH. DIETRICH AND MARIA SIT ON SEPARATE BENCHES FACING ONE ANOTHER. A BAG OF FOOD AND A BOOK SIT NEXT TO MARIA.

DIETRICH

It's good to see you, Maria.

MARIA

Dietrich, how are they treating you?

DIETRICH

I've no cause to complain. The days are long but I have a Bible now. I appreciate the other books you and my parents have sent in. How is your mother?

MARIA

Fine. We're all proud of you.

DIETRICH

I'm proud of her. Thank her from the bottom of my heart for announcing our engagement on the day I was arrested. That's Prussian pluck. I'm hoping I can thank her soon personally.

MARIA

Your father is narrowing the list of possible lawyers.

DIETRICH

Good, but let's not talk about that. Let's think about the wedding and our home. When 1944 starts I'd like to think we'll be in our home, say, in Munich?

MARIA

There's so much to be done yet this year. Just to get you out of here.

DIETRICH

I know, I know. But just for the hope of it we should think of our home from time to time.

MARIA

Of course.

DIETRICH

We should be able to find a small apartment somehow.

Why don't you do some sketches of the rooms? You're a budding artist.

MARIA

I'll bring some sketches the next time I come. Maybe you can work on the menu for our wedding reception. You have such a love for food.

DIETRICH

Do I still show it?

MARIA

You look like you're doing all right.

DIETRICH

I'm meeting all kinds of people here, prisoners from everywhere and not just Germans.

MARIA

The social butterfly even in here.

DIETRICH

My spirits are up, but how I miss you.

TEGEL GUARD 1

Time's almost up.

DIETRICH

We're not permitted to kiss.

MARIA

But we have to!

DIETRICH

We can't!

MARIA

Here's some food. The guards inspected it.

DIETRICH

Thank you.

MARIA

And the book by Stifter that you requested. Your mother found it.

DIETRICH

The Stifter, good. I'll travel through the countryside with Stifter.

MARIA

We'll do it together some day.

DIETRICH

I love you.

MARIA TAKES DIETRICH'S RIGHT HAND
AND WITH THE THUMB AND INDEX
FINGER FORMS A "MOUTH." SHE FORMS
ANOTHER MOUTH, SIMILARLY, WITH HER
OWN RIGHT HAND. SHE BRINGS THE TWO
HANDS TOGETHER AND THEY "HAND
KISS," WHILST FLUTTERING THE
REMAINING FINGERS OF THEIR RIGHT
HANDS. TEGEL GUARD 1 DOESN'T QUITE
KNOW WHAT TO MAKE OF THIS, THEN
ROLLS HIS EYES WITH HIS HANDS HELD
TO HIS HIPS. THE LIGHTS GO OUT. AS THE
LIGHTS GO OUT, THE SOUNDS OF A
HITLER RADIO SPEECH BEGIN TO BE

HEARD. THE RADIO SPEECH CONTINUES
AS THE STAGEHANDS PREPARE
THE NEXT SCENE. MARIA EXITS.

SCENE 2C

SETTING:

WE ARE AT DIETRICH'S ASSIGNED CELL, TEGEL PRISON, IN MID-SUMMER 1943. A BED, A STOOL, AND A PULL-DOWN TABLE ARE THE PRIMARY FURNISHINGS OF DIETRICH'S CELL. THE CELL SHOULD BE PLACED ON TIER 2. THERE ARE BOOKS SCATTERED ABOUT AND ENVELOPES, PAPERS, AND WRITING IMPLEMENTS ON THE TABLE. A BACK WALL MAY HAVE PHO-TOS AND LETTERS AFFIXED TO IT. THERE IS A SMALL OPEN WINDOW, IF POSSIBLE.

AT RISE:

AS THE LIGHTS COME UP, DIETRICH IS SEEN WRITING A LETTER AT HIS DESK. HE IS WEARING A WHITE SHIRT OPEN AT THE TOP. DIETRICH FINISHES AND HIDES THE LETTER AS HE HEARS NOISE OUTSIDE HIS CELL. TEGEL GUARD 1 AND SON-DERKOTHEN ENTER ON TIER 1. SON-DERKOTHEN IS NOT IN UNIFORM. TEGEL GUARD 1 WALKS UP THE STEPS TO DIET-RICH'S CELL AND "OPENS" THE DOOR, SIG-NALING SONDERKOTHEN TO ENTER. AS

SONDERKOTHEN ENTERS THE CELL HE
NODS TO TEGEL GUARD 1, WHO CLICKS HIS
HEELS AND THEN TAKES UP A GUARD POST
OUTSIDE THE DOOR TO DIETRICH'S CELL.

SONDERKOTHEN
Prisoner Bonhoeffer.

DIETRICH
(POPPING TALL)
I am he.

SONDERKOTHEN
And I am Group Leader Sonderkothen, with the SS.

DIETRICH
(EXTENDING HIS HAND)
Welcome to Tegel Military Interrogation Prison. I'm glad
we've met.

SONDERKOTHEN
(DECIDING TO SHAKE DIETRICH'S HAND)
I trust that all is well with you.

DIETRICH
They would be better if I weren't imprisoned but they're
well enough all things considered.

SONDERKOTHEN
Good.

DIETRICH
My family has almost found a lawyer.

SONDERKOTHEN

They've found one. Your father secured a lawyer who before the days of the New Order represented the interests of the Party. Very clever to have picked an old Party member.

DIETRICH

This will insure I'm heard.

SONDERKOTHEN

But to what end? He represents merely you. I represent you and the community. Who should prevail in all fairness? As a Christian you recognize that no community can survive unless the community's needs are kept foremost.

DIETRICH

I'm all for true community.

SONDERKOTHEN

Good. True community is the community of tribe, of race, of blood. Thanks to our leadership Germany is once again achieving true community.

DIETRICH

But community derives from God, from God's love. We—man and woman—are made in the image of God to share that community, to create families from our differences.

SONDERKOTHEN

You are a theologian, of course. Well, I'm a lawyer. And I think you and I can agree that without law, without government, we'd have chaos.

DIETRICH

True enough.

SONDERKOTHEN

Nothing good comes from chaos, yet you seem to have put yourself at odds with the one shield against chaos, the government and the government's laws. I may be a lapsed Christian but I haven't forgotten about St Paul's counsel that Christians ought to obey governments. From the outset of the New Order you have refused the oath of allegiance to Adolf Hitler. You have denied the validity of the Aryan Clause. You have refused to serve Germany in the State Church.

DIETRICH

Is that why I've been held these past three months?

SONDERKOTHEN

No.

DIETRICH

Then why have I been held?

SONDERKOTHEN

We're interested in your church activities. We're interested in your Abwehr activities. Curious that a pastor of the Confessing Church would serve in the Abwehr, don't you think?

DIETRICH

They use all kinds of people, as I gather they must. I was pleased to be of service.

SONDERKOTHEN

I don't know of any other pastors who serve in the Abwehr, even from the State Church.

DIETRICH

The Abwehr uses even Communists and Jews, they tell me. It should be no surprise that they stoop, too, to the likes of me.

SONDERKOTHEN

Maybe. Two days after our Leader's advent to power, back in 1933, you began a radio broadcast with many aspersions on the new leadership.

DIETRICH

The broadcast was cut short.

SONDERKOTHEN

By Party operatives. I could go on and on about you. But among everything I'm drawn to your statement that all who stand apart from the Confessing Church stand apart from salvation. Just what did you mean by that?

DIETRICH

I wasn't directing that statement at Baptists, say, or Catholics. It was directed at my fellow German Evangelicals.

SONDERKOTHEN

It was an insidious remark directed at the State Church.

DIETRICH

I know now to let God be the judge of the State Church. In His mercy it still stands.

SONDERKOTHEN

One way or another over the years we have managed to deal with the pastors of the Confessing Church, many of whom are now dead. Your ability to get about has caused several of us in the security services to wonder how you've managed to keep abroad all these years.

DIETRICH
For some time now I have been under orders from the Gestapo to give no public speeches. And I haven't. And I have been forbidden from entering Berlin except to visit my parents or Abwehr headquarters. You know I haven't violated these restrictions.

SONDERKOTHEN
You're evading the topic—which is how you've managed to keep abroad.

DIETRICH
I've managed because I've done nothing wrong. Indeed, through the Abwehr I believe many would argue I have helped Germany.

SONDERKOTHEN
I'm sure.

DIETRICH
Why should I have chosen to return to my homeland just when war was imminent if I hadn't wanted to help?

SONDERKOTHEN
It doesn't make sense. You are a puzzle but we will put the pieces together.

DIETRICH
(WITH HUMOR)
Perhaps it would all make more sense to you if you thought of me as acting from a love of country. It's not only the government angels who love their country.

SONDERKOTHEN

Government angels! Spare me.

DIETRICH

Forgive me!

SONDERKOTHEN

Do you believe in angels?

DIETRICH

In real angels, yes. They're mentioned throughout the Old and New Testaments, but I've never had what most people would call obvious encounters.

SONDERKOTHEN

You read the Old Testament, do you?

DIETRICH

Of course.

SONDERKOTHEN

You are soiling yourself with the tall tales and money morality of cattle dealers and pimps.

DIETRICH

May Christ forgive you.

SONDERKOTHEN

Christ was against the Jews. If you truly love your country and your religion you would renounce all ties to Jewry, including their infernal book. The book that anchors any society cannot, in any event, be a book of religion. It is the book of laws. As a German citizen, even as an Abwehr agent, you must obey German law. And I remind you that the Leadership is the source of all German law.

DIETRICH

A Christian or Jewish person is not first bound to law, not even God's law, but to God Himself. God's law is a blessing beside God. And man's laws are a blessing, too, but only to the extent they mirror God's law.

SONDERKOTHEN

And who is to hold up the mirror? The Jew community is a snake-pit. No truth will ever arise from them. As for Christians, in the church you obey the hand of men long dead, men enchanted with delusions of a resurrection. Or you're left to be guided by your own conscience, really your own whims. Either way, the professing Christian is a danger to true community. Only the State can bring order to this mess.

WHILE THE FOLLOWING DIALOGUE TAKES PLACE, RECHTER ENTERS STAGE. HE RELIEVES TEGEL GUARD 1, WHO EXITS THE STAGE SET.

DIETRICH

Why even have a State Church?

SONDERKOTHEN

That's a good question, more for you, than for me. If you are to be consistent with your own profession of faith, you should be obedient to the State, as Paul advised.

DIETRICH

So the Bible does have relevance to life?

SONDERKOTHEN

Only for believers.

DIETRICH

I shall pray for a renewal of your faith.

SONDERKOTHEN

Don't bother. God has no ears. We do. We'll be looking forward to hearing more from you. I hope we can talk again, soon. In the meantime, my advice is that you cooperate. Good day, Prisoner Bonhoeffer.

RECHTER CLICKS HIS HEELS
AS SONDERKOTHEN PASSES.

DIETRICH

Good day, Group Leader Sonderkothen.

SONDERKOTHEN EXITS DIETRICH'S
CELL AND EXITS STAGE SET.
RECHTER TURNS TO DIETRICH.

RECHTER

You will be staying, Pastor Bonhoeffer?

DIETRICH

For the time being, Corporal Rechter.

RECHTER

Good.

DIETRICH

I'd rather be out of here.

RECHTER

You could be in worse places.

DIETRICH

The guards have been kind.

RECHTER

Even the worst have lost their rough edges since you've been here.

DIETRICH
(PULLING OUT THE LETTER HE'D
HIDDEN EARLIER, SIGNING IT,
AND SEALING IT IN AN ENVELOPE)

God be praised. Which reminds me. I have another illicit letter for delivery to my friend Eberhard. Would you post it, Corporal Rechter?

RECHTER

I've done this enough that I think you should know my Christian name is Andreas.

DIETRICH

Andreas. That's a fine name. My Christian name is Dietrich.

RECHTER
(TAKING THE LETTER)

Yes, I know. Thank you, Pastor.

RECHTER HIDES THE LETTER UNDER
HIS TUNIC. LIGHTS FADE DOWN
(BUT NOT OUT) ON THE STAGE SET.
RECHTER CAN DELIVER THIS LETTER
TO EBERHARD, WHO WITH MARIA
AND MOTHER, ENTERS THE STAGE
SET WHEN THE LIGHTS ARE FADED.
AS RECHTER EXITS THE STAGE SET,
EBERHARD OPENS THE LETTER.

SCENE 2D

SETTING:

WE ARE IN BERLIN DURING LATE SUM-
MER 1943. THE CELL, ON TIER 2, IS UNAL-
TERED FROM THE PRECEDING SCENE.
TIER 1 AND THE STAGE LEVEL ARE IN THE
BONHOEFFER HOUSE.

AT RISE:

EBERHARD IS SITTING DOWN STAGE,
USING THE TIER 1 DECK AS A CHAIR
ALONG WITH MARIA. MOTHER IS STAND-
ING. EBERHARD IS IN UNIFORM.

EBERHARD
(READING)

I was delighted to learn that you and Renaté are expecting a child.

MARIA

It is wonderful, Eberhard.

EBERHARD

Yes.

(RESUMING HIS READING)
I'm sure in God's grace Renaté will bear a child that will bring great joy to you both and to the family.

WHILE EBERHARD CONTINUES TO READ THE LETTER, FOLLOWING, THE TEGEL SERGEANT ENTERS THE SET, GOES TO DIETRICH'S CELL, AND BEGINS TO SYSTEMATICALLY SEARCH THE CELL—BUT WITHOUT ANIMOSITY. DIETRICH AND THE TEGEL SERGEANT PANTOMIME ANY SPEAKING THAT MIGHT BE IMAGINED IN THIS SITUATION. WHILE DIETRICH FIRST COMES TO ATTENTION WHEN THE TEGEL SERGEANT ENTERS, AS THE SEARCH CONTINUES AND AS DIETRICH AND THE TEGEL SERGEANT "CONVERSE", BOTH BECOME MORE RELAXED. THE SEARCH ENDS SHORTLY BEFORE EBERHARD COMPLETES HIS READING. THE TEGEL SERGEANT EXITS AND DIETRICH SITS ON HIS BUNK, PAGING CAREFULLY FROM BACK TO FRONT IN A BOOK.

MOTHER

Indeed.

EBERHARD
(READING)
I would be less than honest to say I'm indifferent to your plan to name the child Dietrich, if it's a boy.

MOTHER

I should hope he also wouldn't be indifferent if you decided to name a *girl* Dietrich.

THERE IS LAUGHTER ALL AROUND.

EBERHARD
(READING)

I would be quite honored.

(BRIEF PAUSE)

That's what Dietrich writes.

(READING AGAIN)

Neither you nor Renaté should become unduly concerned about your prospective separation. We learn much through adversity. And if you have to be sent somewhere you could do worse than being sent to Italy.

MOTHER

Viva Italia!

MARIA

How Dietrich loves Italy.

EBERHARD
(READING)

I hope you are able to visit Rome and to see the Vatican. Perhaps you may even be able to meet the Pope.

MOTHER

How could that happen?

EBERHARD
(READING)

Keep the Roman Catholic church, too, in your prayers as she struggles with the Modernists all about us. I have been thinking more about the Western church, Catholic and Protestant, and about modern man—not just the Modernists—and I am becoming more and more convinced that we need a religionless Christianity if we are to reach people in the midst of their lives. The church must be less separate from life, more immersed in it. We must refocus the life of the church on this life, not on the next. A preoccupation with the next life is unhealthy; it borders on the irresponsible. I must bring this to a close, yours, Dietrich.

(NOT READING)

Religionless Christianity, hm.

MOTHER

And still no word on the charges underlying his arrest.

EBERHARD

That may show up when we get a book back from him. So far our hiding messages in the books has gone undetected.

MOTHER

I'm going to tell Father you got another letter. Thank you for sharing it with us, Eberhard.

EBERHARD

Of course.

MARIA

We'll keep our heads up.

MOTHER

It's a blessing to have you as part of the family.

MOTHER EXITS.

EBERHARD

I wonder what he means by "religionless Christianity." Would he have us dissolve the church, as the Modernists want?

MARIA

And what *do* the Modernists want...

(BRIEF PAUSE)

...from Dietrich?

LIGHTS OUT ON THE SET.
EBERHARD AND MARIA EXIT.

SCENE 2E

SETTING:

WE ARE AT DIETRICH'S CELL, TEGEL PRISON, IN AUTUMN 1943.

AT RISE:

DIETRICH IS IN HIS CELL, ON TIER 2. HE IS WEARING A SUIT COAT, SWEATER VEST, AND WHITE SHIRT AND IS SMOKING A PIPE AS THE SCENE OPENS. RECHTER AND SONDERKOTHEN ENTER ON TIER 1. SONDERKOTHEN IS NOT IN UNIFORM; HE IS CARRYING A VALISE. RECHTER WALKS UP THE STEPS TO DIETRICH'S CELL AND "OPENS" THE "DOOR." AS RECHTER ENTERS THE CELL HE NODS TO DIETRICH. SONDERKOTHEN ENTERS ON RECHTER'S HEELS.

RECHTER
Attention for Group Leader Sonderkothen.

DIETRICH STANDS AT ATTENTION.

DIETRICH
Group Leader Sonderkothen. Good day.

SONDERKOTHEN
Good day. Dismissed, Corporal.

RECHTER CLICKS HIS HEELS,
THEN EXITS THE STAGE.

SONDERKOTHEN
Please, be seated.

DIETRICH SITS.

DIETRICH
May I ask? Have you finally brought formal charges?

SONDERKOTHEN
You and I need to discuss Operation U7, even though you
have discussed it with my colleagues.

DIETRICH
I've related all the facts as I know them.

SONDERKOTHEN
A lawyer must never be deterred by so-called facts, not
when he is seeking a greater truth. Beneath everyone there
lurk surprises and treasures.

DIETRICH
So?

SONDERKOTHEN

In the modern era, we must be honest with one another. There must be full disclosure, so that we can deal with each other forthrightly.

DIETRICH

Without denying the need for honesty, there is also a need for privacy. Human beings left without some measure of privacy soon are left without dignity, they are treated inhumanely.

SONDERKOTHEN

Am I hearing Bonhoeffer the theologian or Bonhoeffer the politician?

DIETRICH

I have never been a politician.

SONDERKOTHEN

If you had erected a wall between your religion and your public life, I would believe you. But your theology is inherently political, since it intrudes into the business of the State.

DIETRICH

Especially as you define the State.

SONDERKOTHEN

In your theology does the State have a proper interest in financial irregularities?

DIETRICH

Yes.

SONDERKOTHEN

Your brother-in-law, Hans, is suspected of financial irregularities in connection with Operation U7. Your sister, Christine, has a taste for high living. High living means low cash unless there's a cow about. We believe your brother milked money from the Jews in Operation U7 as the price for setting them up as so-called "spies" in Switzerland.

DIETRICH

That's preposterous.

SONDERKOTHEN

We've arrested a German businessman who has confessed to receiving money for his assistance in setting up these Jews.

DIETRICH

I wouldn't know anything about that.

SONDERKOTHEN

Wouldn't it have occurred to you there was something strange in the Abwehr's using Jews, for God's sake, as spies in Switzerland?

DIETRICH

On the contrary, I thought it was very clever. Who would think the New Order would use Jewish persons as spies? They've probably been quite effective at ferreting out information about Swiss military installations.

SONDERKOTHEN

Spare me. You made trips to Switzerland to visit these spies, after they were put in place.

DIETRICH

I traveled there under cover of doing business for the World Alliance of Churches, as I've told the others, but, yes, I did canvass these spies for information, information I merely passed along in sealed envelopes. I was never privy to the contents of these envelopes.

SONDERKOTHEN

And your brother-in-law and sister? You never shared in their payoffs?

DIETRICH

Hans and Christine are loyal Germans. I'm certain they would never have milked Abwehr agents for payoffs.

SONDERKOTHEN

These were Jews, for Christ's sake.

DIETRICH

You shouldn't use the Lord's name in vain, even if you don't believe in Him.

SONDERKOTHEN

I'm not here to be lectured on how to talk. You may be able to talk to me with impunity now, but I assure you you will not be released until I'm satisfied you're innocent. If you had been in a Gestapo prison, long ago I would have had the resources to determine your guilt or innocence.

DIETRICH

I'm glad enough to be in an Army prison.

SONDERKOTHEN

Of that, I'm sure.

(BRIEF PAUSE)
I do hear all kinds of stories about your conduct here.

DIETRICH SHRUGS AND OPENS OUT HIS HANDS TOWARDS SONDERKOTHEN.

SONDERKOTHEN
If you were as well behaved out of prison as in, you'd be a hero of the Realm.

DIETRICH
Really?

SONDERKOTHEN
I'm told during air raids the guards and prisoners want to be with you. You are fearless, I'm told.

DIETRICH
I am merely human. Any fearlessness they see in me is a gift from God to them.

SONDERKOTHEN
Are you ashamed of your fearlessness? A man should be proud, not humble. Modern man should never fear to take credit where credit is due, to take responsibility where responsibility must be taken. Your irresponsibility about your own courage—something people around you admire—serves to confirm me in my belief that Christianity—like Judaism—is a sham, a void hidden by a pretense of profundity. Your religion becomes an excuse for doing anything and hiding a lot. I wouldn't be at all surprised if you have engaged in great treachery while truly believing you had done no wrong at all.

DIETRICH

Both shame and courage are gifts from God. My responsibility is not to take credit for these gifts but to use them. With courage I bring hope to others and to myself. And with shame I bring myself into God's presence. Without shame, without humility, we cannot live before God. And without God we can no longer be human.

SONDERKOTHEN

Live before God! As if your God were hiding just behind the clouds.

DIETRICH

You would have it so, but He is right here in our midst.

SONDERKOTHEN

He, too, must be ashamed. I can't see him.

DIETRICH

We could not stand His full radiance in this life. That would be the end of history. But God has revealed Himself, starting with Abraham and Sarah, most fully in His Son, and even still through His Holy Spirit.

SONDERKOTHEN

A childish, Jew mutant of a cult! Yours is not a man's god.

DIETRICH

And your god, now, what is his nature?

SONDERKOTHEN

God is not a him; whatever some might call god. God is the creative principle of this world. But this creative process is not human in any way—that's a problem that Jews and Christians have created for themselves. They make God in their own image. But God, the creative force, does not hear and cannot see.

DIETRICH
But he speaks through our Leader?

SONDERKOTHEN
Your ridicule is dangerous. Don't be seduced by the power of words. You may ridicule the Leadership, but who has the power over whether you live or die? The only thing that counts in this world—which our Leader appreciates—is action. He who would make this world a better place must act, must succeed whatever the sacrifice. There are no other guides to human behavior.

DIETRICH
Yes, the results are obvious. Without God history is conditioned on accident and whim.

SONDERKOTHEN
You make history without God sound capricious. But there is human will, which conditions nature and humanity. And from the will comes progress.

DIETRICH
And evil.

SONDERKOTHEN
The problem of man is the problem of bringing a diversity of wills into concert to create the good, the beautiful, the true. Practically speaking that means people must be selected out who are ugly, evil, dishonest, or stupid.

DIETRICH

The problem of man is that he must bring his will into subservience to God's will, otherwise man will never attain what is truly beautiful or good.

SONDERKOTHEN

You continue to bring your God into the picture.

DIETRICH

He is inescapable.

SONDERKOTHEN

For the cowardly or the intellectually deficient. Look at science. Is God needed there?

DIETRICH

Can mankind survive on science alone? Science is not wisdom.

SONDERKOTHEN

You evade my question.

DIETRICH

All right, scientific culture marginalizes God. If God is invoked He is merely brought in to answer unanswered questions.

SONDERKOTHEN

I couldn't have said it better. With time there will be fewer and fewer unanswered questions. To be sure, there will always be the unanswered questions, a part of God, if you will. But practically speaking, mankind is the center of history.

DIETRICH

You and your party are thoroughly modern: self-made men worshipping anything but God.

SONDERKOTHEN

Not really. We put faith in science.

(PAUSE)

And in our Leadership.

DIETRICH

What's the connection between the two?

SONDERKOTHEN

The great man, who is now Adolf Hitler. He is laying the foundation for the next millennium.

DIETRICH
(OVERLAPPING)

Thank heavens, life is short.

SONDERKOTHEN

He is bringing honesty of vision and resoluteness of purpose to building a new Europe. Under him there is hope of achieving a society where reasonable men, instead of greedy scum, will have the upper hand, where beauty and not cheap commercialism will prevail.

DIETRICH

In Germany we have a long way to go in achieving these goals.

SONDERKOTHEN

So you recognize that?

DIETRICH

It is quite apparent the Party stands in the forefront of modernism. I just wish the Party would recognize there are those of us, from older, perhaps obsolete, traditions who wish to serve Germany in ways suited to our more limited visions.

SONDERKOTHEN

But that is the point. The greatest vision must inform all if we are to evolve to the greatest society.

DIETRICH

In that spirit I have entirely deferred to my betters at the Abwehr. Can I be held accountable if they chose to place Jewish spies in Switzerland?

SONDERKOTHEN

Yes, well, to spare you anxieties about the Abwehr's leadership, you will remain in detention in this prison indefinitely. Here of all places, your calling as a Christian and as a citizen seem to have met. I am passing on to my superiors all these reports about how you are boosting the morale of prisoners and staff alike. They even say you do a splendid job of bandaging up people in the infirmary. Keep up the good work, Prisoner Bonhoeffer. You should be proud of it.

DIETRICH

Thank you Group Leader Sonderkothen.

SONDERKOTHEN

Good day.

DIETRICH

Good day.

SONDERKOTHEN EXITS CELL AND
THENCE THE STAGE SET. RECHTER
ENTERS, GOING TO DIETRICH'S CELL,
WHOSE "DOOR" HE "OPENS."

RECHTER

How did it go?

DIETRICH

Not good.

RECHTER

Are you to be sent elsewhere?

DIETRICH

I don't know. I'm to be held indefinitely. They'll hold me
until they find some reason to confirm their suspicions. It's
only a matter of time before they loose patience.

RECHTER

You must think of how to get out of here.

DIETRICH

How else but through a Party-affiliated lawyer, my good
Rechter?

RECHTER

Escape.

LIGHTS DOWN ON THE SET. EBERHARD
ENTERS THE STAGE AT A DISTANCE
FROM DIETRICH AND RECHTER. A
SPOTLIGHT UP ON EBERHARD, READING
ANOTHER LETTER FROM DIETRICH.

EBERHARD

...so it is with the passing of time I find more and more comfort in reading the Old Testament. In part, I've decided one cannot appreciate the New Testament of our Lord Jesus Christ without understanding what it means to serve and love God without Christ. Partly, I find comfort in the prophets of old, now most especially Moses, whose work for God has become a model, in some ways, of what I must do.

LIGHTS DOWN ON EBERHARD. RECHTER AND EBERHARD EXIT THE STAGE. AS THE STAGEHANDS CHANGE THE SET, GERMAN CHRISTMAS CAROLS AND HYMNS ARE PLAYED UNTIL THE TEGEL SERGEANT TURNS OFF THE RADIO IN THE NEXT SCENE.

SCENE 2F

SETTING:

WE ARE AT TEGEL PRISON ON CHRISTMAS EVE, 1943. AS IN **SCENE 2B**, ABOVE, THE STAGE LEVEL IS SET AS A VISITORS' ROOM. ADDITIONALLY, TIER 1 IS SET UP AS A RECEPTION OFFICE. ON TIER 1 THERE IS A DESK AND CHAIR, A NAZI FLAG ON A POLE SET IN A STAND, AND A PORTRAIT OF ADOLF HITLER. THERE IS A RADIO ON THE DESK AND OTHER PARAPHERNALIA, AS APPROPRIATE. TIER 2 THROUGHOUT THIS SCENE IS KEPT DARK OR OBSCURED.

AT RISE:

AS LIGHTS COME UP ON TIER 1, WE SEE THE TEGEL SERGEANT SITTING AT HIS DESK WRITING OR TYPING A REPORT. AS MARIA ENTERS THE STAGE, THE TEGEL SERGEANT FLIPS OFF THE RADIO SET, WHICH HAS BEEN HEARD PLAYING CHRISTMAS MUSIC. MARIA ENTERS THE STAGE HAULING, PERHAPS DRAGGING, AN EVERGREEN TREE.

TEGEL SERGEANT
My God in heaven, what have we got here?

MARIA
A Christmas tree.

TEGEL SERGEANT
And what is the meaning of that?

MARIA
To celebrate Christ's birth, of course.

TEGEL SERGEANT
I know that.

MARIA
And death and resurrection.

TEGEL SERGEANT
I know that, too. But you can't bring a Christmas tree in here.

MARIA
It's not for right here, it's for my fiancé, Pastor Bonhoeffer.

TEGEL SERGEANT
Ah, yes, I should have recognized you. You startled me with that tree.

MARIA
It's beautiful, isn't it? The man who sold it to me said it came from the Harz forests.

TEGEL SERGEANT
(LIFTING UP THE TELEPHONE HANDSET)
All that way!

(SPEAKING INTO THE HANDSET)
Bring Prisoner Bonhoeffer, quickly.

(TO MARIA)
How far did you carry it?

MARIA
I only had to change trolleys once.

TEGEL SERGEANT
By trolley, no less. Did you have to pay an extra fare?

MARIA
Not at all. The conductor winked at the tree.

TEGEL SERGEANT
That I can understand, but I can't let you give that tree to
Pastor Bonhoeffer, as much as I'd like to. I have sent some-
one to fetch him from the infirmary.

MARIA
He's just working there, of course?

TEGEL SERGEANT
Of course. He's a good man, which is why I'm going to
let you see him. You know this is all quite irregular.

MARIA
It's kind of you.

TEGEL SERGEANT

No hugging or kissing at all, otherwise we'll have to search for weapons and suicide pills.

MARIA

I understand.

MARIA IS STILL HOLDING THE CHRISTMAS TREE. IT IS IN A POSITION TO OBSCURE HER TO DIETRICH, WHO NOW ENTERS ESCORTED BY RECHTER.

TEGEL SERGEANT

Ah, Pastor Bonhoeffer.

DIETRICH

Sergeant. Good evening.

MARIA
(PEEKING AROUND THE TREE)

Hey! What about me?

DIETRICH

Maria, how wonderful to see you! How did you get here?

MARIA

I thought you might like a Christmas tree in your cell.

TEGEL SERGEANT

God in heaven!

DIETRICH

I would, but that isn't permitted.

MARIA

The sergeant just told me...after all this way.

TEGEL SERGEANT

Yes.

DIETRICH

I can't think of a better Christmas present.

MARIA

I'm glad you like it. Perhaps the men down here can keep it for you.

DIETRICH

What do you think, Sergeant?

TEGEL SERGEANT

I think...I think...I think that would be fine. Thank you very much, madam. Yes, just leave the tree, here, against my desk. The two of you may have a brief visit in the visitors' area and then I will have to ask you to leave, madam. Rechter, please show Pastor Bonhoeffer and his fiancée to the visitors' room. They're in your custody. Five minutes.

LIGHTS UP ON THE STAGE LEVEL. LIGHTS DIMMED ON TIER 1. RECHTER ESCORTS DIETRICH TO A BENCH, WITH MARIA FOLLOWING. DIETRICH AND MARIA SIT OPPOSITE ONE ANOTHER ON THE BENCHES. RECHTER AWKWARDLY ASSUMES THE ROLE OF WATCHMAN. TEGEL SERGEANT EXITS STAGE.

DIETRICH

I don't suppose this has ever happened before at Tegel Prison. You're amazing.

RECHTER TURNS AWAY TO LISTEN
FOR ANYONE COMING.

MARIA

I couldn't let Christmas go by without doing something.

DIETRICH

You are a Godsend, Maria. I love you.

MARIA

What I wouldn't give for the day when you're out.

DIETRICH

Maria, this is Corporal Andreas Rechter, the man I referred to in my most recent book message. He's the one who's offered to help me escape in work clothes.

RECHTER TURNS, APPROACHES MARIA,
AND EXTENDS A HAND,
WHICH SHE TAKES IN BOTH HANDS.

MARIA

Oh, thank you. Thank you.

RECHTER
(SHAKING, THEN DISENGAGING)
A pleasure to meet you Miss Wedemeyer. I must...

RECHTER NODS, MARIA NODS, AND
RECHTER RESUMES A POSITION
PREPARED TO ALERT DIETRICH AND
MARIA OF ANYONE'S COMING. MARIA
RESUMES HER POSITION ON THE
BENCH OPPOSITE DIETRICH.

DIETRICH

He'll be coming with me. I'm convinced we should go to the south, in Germany. Rechter and I are working on the details. Tell my family that as soon as we've settled on the details, I'll get that information to you all, through Andreas. He's a good man. This will all be quite dangerous. If I stay here, perhaps there's a chance of my living. But if he and I are caught, we'll both be finished...and perhaps others, too. Are you...

MARIA

Don't worry about me. If we do nothing you'll soon be dead. I'd rather die than live without you.

THE TEGEL SERGEANT AND TEGEL
GUARD 1 ENTER, WALKING TOWARD
THE "VISITORS' ROOM."

RECHTER

Pastor, Pastor, they're coming.

RECHTER RESUMES THE POST HE
SHOULD HAVE BEEN IN, NAMELY
WATCHING OVER DIETRICH AND MARIA,
WHO ASSUME A MANNER CUSTOMARY
IN THE VISITORS' ROOM.

DIETRICH
God bless you, Maria.

MARIA
(QUICKLY SHOWING DIETRICH A "HAND KISS")
He has. And may He continue to bless you.

DIETRICH STARTS TO FORM HIS HAND
INTO A "HAND KISS", BUT FEARING DIS-
COVERY BY THE INCOMING GUARDS,
RETURNS HIS HAND TO THE BENCH.

RECHTER
(CRACKING A SMILE)
Bless us everyone.

DIETRICH AND MARIA
Yes.

THE TEGEL SERGEANT AND TEGEL
GUARD 1 ARRIVE, RECHTER COMES TO
ATTENTION AND CLICKS HIS HEELS, AND
THE LIGHTS GO OUT ON THE SET. TEGEL
SERGEANT, TEGEL GUARD 1, AND MARIA
EXIT.

SCENE 2G

SETTING:

WE ARE AT DIETRICH'S CELL, TEGEL PRISON, IN JULY 1944 AND EARLY OCTOBER 1944. THE CELL MAY HAVE AN ADDITIONAL ACCUMULATION OF BOOKS, PAPERS, PHOTOS, ETC. AS THE SET PERMITS, TO SHOW THE PASSAGE OF PRISON TIME. IF THE CELL HAS A WINDOW, IT IS OPEN. WITH A WINDOW IT WOULD BE APPROPRIATE TO HEAR THE SOUNDS OF BIRDS, PERHAPS BEGINNING AFTER THE LIGHTS GO OUT ON THE PREVIOUS SCENE AND IN ANY EVENT FADING OUT WHEN THE LIGHTS COME UP ON THIS SCENE.

AT RISE:

AS THE LIGHTS COME UP ON TIERS 1 AND 2, DIETRICH IS READING A LETTER. HE IS PACING BACK AND FORTH, SUCH AS HIS ACCOMMODATION PERMITS. RECHTER IS ENTERING THE STAGE SET ON TIER 1. RECHTER WALKS UP TO DIETRICH'S CELL, KNOCKS ON THE "DOOR", AND ENTERS.

> RECHTER

A good letter from Eberhard?

> DIETRICH

Yes, good. From this will come a lot of good "conversations," if you know what I mean.

> RECHTER

I know what you mean.

> (BRIEF PAUSE)

I've got some news.

> DIETRICH

What is it?

> RECHTER

Your uncle just pulled up.

> DIETRICH

Uncle who?

> RECHTER

General Von Hase. I'd better go.

> RECHTER EXITS. DIETRICH BEGINS
> PACING. THE TEGEL SERGEANT ENTERS,
> WALKING RAPIDLY TO DIETRICH'S CELL.
> THE SERGEANT KNOCKS AT DIETRICH'S
> CELL "DOOR," THEN ENTERS.

TEGEL SERGEANT

Pastor Bonhoeffer, forgive me for interrupting you but the Military Commandant of Berlin is here. You're to meet with him and Prison Commandant Maetz in Captain Maetz's office.

DIETRICH

Uncle Paul, here?

TEGEL SERGEANT

Yes.

UNCLE PAUL ENTERS WALKING TO DIETRICH'S CELL. IF THERE ARE EXTRAS AVAILABLE, IT WOULD BE APPROPRIATE FOR UNCLE PAUL TO BE ESCORTED BY AN AIDE-DE-CAMP, WHO WOULD POST HIMSELF OUTSIDE DIETRICH'S CELL.

TEGEL SERGEANT

He may be Uncle Paul to you but he is General Commandant von Hase to me.

DIETRICH

I assure you...

TEGEL SERGEANT
(POPPING TO ATTENTION AND SALUTING)
Attention! Hail Victory!

UNCLE PAUL RETURNS THE PARTY SALUTE WITH AN OLD-FASHIONED MILITARY SALUTE.

UNCLE PAUL
(ENTERING DIETRICH'S CELL)

At ease, Sergeant. You may tell Commandant Maetz that Prisoner Bonhoeffer and I will be in his office shortly.

TEGEL SERGEANT

Yes, sir. By your leave, sir.

UNCLE PAUL

Granted.

TEGEL SERGEANT EXITS.

UNCLE PAUL

Dietrich, I apologize. You've been in here over a year now and this is the first time I've visited you.

DIETRICH
(SHAKING HANDS)

Uncle Paul. Should you even be in here now? I've never expected a visit from you.

UNCLE PAUL

From everything I've heard, you're not a man easily frightened.

(BRIEF PAUSE)

It's hot in here.

DIETRICH

May I offer you some water?

UNCLE PAUL

On the contrary, in Captain Maetz's office we'll all have some wine I brought. I think you'll enjoy it.

DIETRICH

Wine?

UNCLE PAUL

It's still available. But we haven't much time for business before pleasure.

DIETRICH

What business?

UNCLE PAUL

You'll know what I mean. July 1944 will be a volatile month before it's all over.

DIETRICH

I see.

UNCLE PAUL

And I'm concerned.

DIETRICH

About a volatile enterprise?

UNCLE PAUL

About it's failing.

DIETRICH

You're the one who's brave. How many battles have you been in? How many times shot?

UNCLE PAUL

The courage required of a hammer is different than the courage required of a rope. In battle one is flailed about so much there's nothing else but to be brave. But in the quiet before battle, one's nerves are stretched to the limit. One's imagination has so much opportunity to think of what can go wrong.

DIETRICH

That you serve a righteous cause should give you some comfort. Jesus promises...

UNCLE PAUL

Forgive me, Dietrich, but I'm Christian in hardly more than name.

DIETRICH

I've often suspected as much. Is there anything I can say or do to show you Christ's mercy?

UNCLE PAUL

It's too late in life for that.

DIETRICH

Until you're dead it's never too late.

UNCLE PAUL

Maybe. But I've had plenty of opportunity to think about death these last months, these last years. I see death every day in Berlin.

DIETRICH

As in battle.

UNCLE PAUL

But war deaths are never so bad as the other kind, the ones I see here in Berlin, deaths at the hands of you-know-who.

DIETRICH

The Modernists have perfected so many ways of torture.

UNCLE PAUL

Both retail and wholesale. They have caused me to think more about hell than I ever had and now about heaven and God—more than I ever thought I would.

DIETRICH

Are you wondering how God can permit this hell on earth?

UNCLE PAUL

No. The fact that I recognize hell on earth has made me inclined to think there is a moral God after all. Why should I know this is hell?

DIETRICH

God has not abandoned you, even in the midst of the freedom he grants all.

UNCLE PAUL

You think so?

DIETRICH

That is a constant theme in the Bible, both in the Old and New Testaments.

UNCLE PAUL

For you these things always have seemed so straightforward. For coming from such a brainy family, you are like a child in your belief.

DIETRICH

As God would have it, you are His child, too.

UNCLE PAUL

I've become too much to be a child. A child is irresponsible. I'm a grown man and you are, too. You've taken responsibility and we're all proud of you for it.

DIETRICH

I'd like to think so. But I would never want to suggest the images in the Bible are meant as licenses for irresponsibility. They are calls, like battle flags, to be loyal and responsible to God, our creator. To be a child of God is to grow as much as we ever can in this life, in obedience to God. If following a flag in battle is a responsible thing—and it is—it is a manly thing. It is an obedient thing. Why balk at being obedient to God? To be obedient to God is both childlike and mature. It is to be most fully human.

UNCLE PAUL

But I can't accept all the Christian baggage—the church, the doctrines, the obligations—that you accept as a matter of course.

DIETRICH

Christ brings us the yoke we can bear. The church, even with all its baggage...

UNCLE PAUL

The dissension, too?

DIETRICH

That, too, is something we must bear, for Christ's sake.

UNCLE PAUL

I'm not fit for the church.

DIETRICH

Yes, I often think of your likes. Knowing what I know now, I think I must pray for you anew.

UNCLE PAUL

Right now? We need to get going.

DIETRICH
(IN GOOD HUMOR)

I meant later.

UNCLE PAUL

Prayer is not something I can do.

DIETRICH

Perhaps you're coming here was a prayer.

UNCLE PAUL

Perhaps. I'm still uncomfortable.

DIETRICH

With God or with this July enterprise?

UNCLE PAUL

With both.

DIETRICH

And God is uncomfortable, too. We all sin and that grieves God. The duty of a Christian is to be a servant of God by being faithful, hopeful, loving. To you, I think Christ would say, as He said in his Sermon on the Mount, "Blessed are those who hunger and thirst for righteousness, for they shall be satisfied." Christ puts not one word of condition in that blessing. No one has to be a Christian to receive that blessing from God. Christian or not, if you thirst and hunger for righteousness, you shall be satisfied. That is a promise from God.

UNCLE PAUL

Thank you, Dietrich. Thank you. We'd better go.

LIGHTS DOWN ON THE STAGE SET.
UNCLE PAUL EXITS (WITH EXTRA).
DIETRICH PUTS ON A SWEATER OR COAT
JACKET, APPROPRIATE FOR AUTUMN.
DIETRICH SITS AT HIS CELL DESK.
RECHTER ENTERS STAGE SET, TAKING A
POSITION AT DIETRICH'S CELL "DOOR."
AS THE LIGHTS COME UP, DIETRICH IS
SEEN PREPARING A SMALL PACKET.

DIETRICH

Here's the tobacco packet and pipe I want you to deliver to Hoffmann, is it?

RECHTER

Yes, Hoffmann.

DIETRICH

Young fellow, is he?

RECHTER

Twenty-two. He's been on the Eastern Front over three years. Lot's of decorations. One too many battles, I guess, and he lost his head. Ran away, then turned himself in.

DIETRICH

I'm sorry I don't have cigarettes, as he wants. The pipe and tobacco will have to do. I've written a brief meditation, too, to pass along, if he seems inclined to want one. Don't press it on him. You know, my Uncle Paul gave me that pipe in 1930 as a going-away present the first time I went to the States.

RECHTER

General von Hase was a fine officer and a fine man.

DIETRICH

At least when they executed him, they did it fast. Not one of those piano-wire hangings so favored last July. I couldn't take the pain of hanging for a long time. I hate pain.

RECHTER

Don't think of those hangings, Pastor. You won't be getting anywhere near a hangman's noose.

DIETRICH

You still have everything in readiness for us, don't you?

RECHTER

We should try for it in the next few days. It isn't going to get any better.

DIETRICH

You have been so good, Andreas. You've done so much, risked so much. But I tell you we can't think anymore about my escaping here.

RECHTER

Why? Why not?

DIETRICH
(HOLDING UP A BOOK)
I've just learned through this book my mother sent—you brought it up earlier today—that Klaus has been arrested, along with one of my brothers in law and some other people. The Gestapo has found some damaging papers. If I were to escape now, I would endanger Klaus and others. With the Party angry because of the July attempt on Mr Hitler's life, you can be sure Maria and my parents would be arrested and perhaps tortured to death if I were to escape. I cannot put them in harm's way.

RECHTER
Must this be?

DIETRICH
It must.

(PAUSE)

RECHTER
So be it.

DIETRICH
(HANDING OVER THE ITEMS FOR DELIVERY)
Better deliver this stuff. Don't forget to bleach the pipe stem. It's a matter of showing respect; the man doesn't even know me.

RECHTER
I'll take care of it. I'm sure he'll appreciate these things.

DIETRICH
When's his execution?

RECHTER

In two days.

DIETRICH

I'll be praying for him.

(PAUSE)

Andreas, I'll never forget your kindness and courage. Thank you.

RECHTER

I'd better go.

RECHTER EXITS. DIETRICH KNEELS,
ASSUMING A POSTURE OF PRAYER.
LIGHTS FADE OUT ON THE SET.

SCENE 2H

SETTING:

WE ARE AT THE COMMANDANT'S OFFICE,
TEGEL PRISON, LATER IN OCTOBER 1944.
A DESK, CHAIRS, AND OTHER FURNISH-
ING BEFITTING A PRISON COMMAN-
DANT'S OFFICE OCCUPY TIER 1. TIER 2
MAY STILL CONTAIN DIETRICH'S CELL,
BUT IT MUST BE KEPT DARK.

AT RISE:

AS THE LIGHTS COME UP ON THE SET WE
SEE DIETRICH SITTING IN A CHAIR. SON-
DERKOTHEN IS SITTING ON THE CORNER
OF THE DESK. HE IS IN HIS SS UNIFORM,
MINUS HIS CAP, WHICH IS ON THE DESK.

SONDERKOTHEN

I wouldn't worry about charges coming out of the U7
affair anymore.

DIETRICH

Oh?

SONDERKOTHEN

As a result of the assassination attempt the Gestapo and SS through a series of interviews discovered documents cataloguing conspiracies and other traitorous activities, going back at least to 1938. Your brother-in-law, Hans von Dohnanyi, authored these documents.

DIETRICH

That's silly.

SONDERKOTHEN

Less silly with each passing day. One reason I'm here is to tell you your brother, Klaus, and your brother-in-law, Rudiger Schleicher, are in prison because of the new revelations.

DIETRICH

Yes, so now Klaus and Rudiger, too.

SONDERKOTHEN

There are others besides. You don't seem upset about this.

DIETRICH

I am. I won't rest easy until all our names are cleared.

SONDERKOTHEN

I think you'll rest together before you rest easy. Your name appears in Dohnanyi's documents, Bonhoeffer. They refer to a trip you made to Sigtuna, Sweden, in May, 1942, under Abwehr auspices. There you met with a Bishop George Bell, of the Church of England. In that capacity he is also a member of the House of Lords. You discussed with him British government support for the rebel group plotting to replace our nation's leadership. Do you deny that this meeting took place?

DIETRICH

No, not in the least.

SONDERKOTHEN
(STANDING)

Not in the least! You realize that by admitting to participating in this affair, you have admitted to participating in a conspiracy against the German Government. That is high treason, punishable by death.

DIETRICH

But the SS and the Gestapo are too smart to sentence me to death.

SONDERKOTHEN

The audacity!

DIETRICH

I should think that Heinrich Himmler would be pleased to learn of my peace-making efforts on behalf of Germany.

SONDERKOTHEN

You're a bigger fool than I thought.

DIETRICH

I was merely ahead of my time.

SONDERKOTHEN

Spare me.

DIETRICH

For years we've been hearing about the struggle against Bolshevism. I became convinced our leaders would entertain peace-making with the Western powers.

SONDERKOTHEN

Your peace-making efforts were to benefit a rebel government.

DIETRICH

A German government.

SONDERKOTHEN

Don't stretch the matter for a few extra days of your life.

DIETRICH

I have knowledge of parties in the British government who, fearing a Stalin tyranny across Europe, would be pleased to have peace with Germany.

SONDERKOTHEN

Your contacts can't be that extensive.

DIETRICH

Would you want to pass up the opportunity to inform Mr Himmler of a possible avenue to solving a difficult national question?

SONDERKOTHEN

Why should anyone believe you? Your patriotism is non-existent.

DIETRICH

Then I guess you can be done with me.

SONDERKOTHEN

Not quite yet. You are to be transferred to the Reich High Security Office prison. You'll be there along with Admiral Canaris, who has also been arrested.

(SHOUTING)
Guards!

DIETRICH
He, too, can be of help as Germany seeks peace.

SONDERKOTHEN
I remind you, it is treason to even suggest peace.

DIETRICH
It would be stupidity not to consider peace. When I'm at the Reich High Security Office, I'll do all I can to aid peace.

SONDERKOTHEN
(GRABBING HIS CAP)
How you wriggle and writhe! But you will never be a butterfly. You won't escape.

TEGEL GUARD 2 ENTERS.

DIETRICH
I hope our next discussion can be more theological.

SONDERKOTHEN
Never underestimate the power of vengeance.

(TO TEGEL GUARD 2)
Return that prisoner to his cell.

SONDERKOTHEN EXITS.

TEGEL GUARD 2
Yes, sir.

(BRIEF PAUSE)

An unpleasant man.

DIETRICH
(STANDING)

Just one of many modern angels of death.

TEGEL GUARD 2

Trouble comes in spades, Pastor. I have some unpleasant news. Corporal Rechter was killed—in last night's air raid.

LIGHTS OUT ON THE SET.
TEGEL GUARD 2 EXITS. THE
STAGEHANDS CLEAR THE SET AS
A SOUNDTRACK PLAYS OUT THE
MOANS OF ONE PRISONER BEING
BEATEN AND THE MUFFLED
SCREAMS OF ANOTHER FOR MERCY.

SCENE 21

SETTING:

WE ARE AT THE REICH HIGH SECURITY OFFICE ("RHSO"), IN BERLIN, FEBRUARY 1945. TIER 2 IS BEREFT OF DIETRICH'S CELL. TIER 1 AND THE STAGE LEVEL ARE BEREFT OF FURNISHINGS; THEY NOW REPRESENT GANGWAYS IN THE PRISON IN THE BOWELS OF THE RHSO. AS SUCH THEY ARE DIMLY LIT.

AT RISE:

THE SOUNDTRACK FADES AWAY AS THE LIGHTS COME UP ON THE STAGE LEVEL AND TIER 1. CANARIS IS SCRUBBING THE TIER 1 DECK AND DIETRICH IS SCRUB-BING THE STAGE LEVEL DECK. THEY ARE ON THEIR HANDS AND KNEES. BOTH ARE IN PRISON UNIFORM AND EQUIPPED WITH BUCKETS AND SCRUB CLOTHS. RHSO GUARD (A MEMBER OF THE SS) ENTERS ON TIER 1, WALKING TO CANARIS.

RHSO GUARD
Didn't you learn anything in the Navy, swabby? This deck

is filthy. I'm cutting your rations in half tonight.

RHSO GUARD THROWS A CIGARETTE BUTT ONTO CANARIS'S HEAD.

RHSO GUARD
Get to work or you won't be eating anything at all.

CANARIS
Yes, sir.

RHSO GUARD EXITS.

DIETRICH
Admiral Canaris, you are Admiral Canaris, aren't you?

CANARIS
Yes.

DIETRICH
Sorry, sometimes I can't be sure what I see. The lack of food seems to be giving me hallucinations. Don't let them break your spirit, Admiral.

CANARIS
Who are you?

DIETRICH
I was an Abwehr agent. Bonhoeffer's my name.

CANARIS
Pastor Bonhoeffer. You went abroad for us—helped get some people out.

DIETRICH

That's right. One of my brothers-in-law was your chief legal counsel, Hans von Dohnanyi.

CANARIS

Oh, yes. He's the one that brought you into the organization. And he betrayed us.

DIETRICH

Betrayed us? I can't believe that.

CANARIS

He most certainly did. He was right in the thick of one of the plots to kill Chancellor Hitler.

DIETRICH

But he betrayed the Resistance? I can't believe...

CANARIS

Not the Resistance. Germany. He betrayed Germany.

DIETRICH

But, Admiral, your own bureau was a center of the Resistance. You knew everything, didn't you!

CANARIS

I was playing a double game until the time came when it would be appropriate to disclose the conspiracy to the authorities. They won't believe me.

DIETRICH

I don't think I can, either.

CANARIS

I shouldn't have to die for what I've done. I've always

been a patriot.

DIETRICH

No one would blame you for wanting to live. There is so much to live for.

CANARIS

But now I'm stuck in this mess. Unless I get out, it'll get worse.

DIETRICH

The government is collapsing. There is hope.

CANARIS

We're to be transferred to a death camp soon.

DIETRICH

Which one?

CANARIS

Buchenwald, Flossenberg, I don't know.

DIETRICH

Neither has a good reputation. At least we'll get out of doors and farther from the cauldron that's Berlin. We'll be able to see birds.

CANARIS

I don't care about fresh air and birds! If you want to live you've got to think success, Bonhoeffer.

DIETRICH

I'm game if you come up with a plan of escape, but don't put your faith in success.

CANARIS

Why shouldn't I? It's got me through before.

DIETRICH

To where?

CANARIS

Do you have any right to ask?

DIETRICH

Forgive me. Think of life, yes, but take comfort that this life isn't everything. Here's a hunk of bread; you look famished.

CANARIS

Your words contradict your actions.

DIETRICH

I don't have time to explain. Think of it as one of life's pleasant puzzles. You are a master of puzzles, yes?

CANARIS

Yes, yes, I guess I am. How did you get this?

CANARIS BEGINS TO GNAW AT THE BREAD.

DIETRICH

My fiancée delivered some yesterday. They allow relatives now to bring food. Take it.

CANARIS BEGINS TO RETURN
THE BREAD TO DIETRICH.

DIETRICH

Keep it.

RHSO GUARD ENTERS.

CANARIS

I will live!

RHSO GUARD

Get to work, you two. Traitors are not permitted to be slackers!

CANARIS HIDES THE BREAD HUNK.
DIETRICH RESUMES WORK. LIGHTS
DOWN ON THE SET. CANARIS AND
RHSO GUARD EXIT. A SOUNDTRACK
OF MOANING IS HEARD.

SCENE 2J

SETTING:

WE ARE AT DIETRICH'S CELL IN THE RHSO IN FEBRUARY 1945. THE CELL AMOUNTS TO NOTHING MORE THAN A SPOTLIT AREA ON THE STAGE LEVEL. THERE IS A BOOK ON THE STAGE AS WELL AS A LEATHER OR CLOTH BAG WITH POUCHES.

AT RISE:

SPOTLIGHTS ARE ON DIETRICH SLEEPING IN HIS RHSO CELL, WITH A BOOK AND BAG NEARBY. AS THE SOUNDTRACK FADES, THE RHSO GUARD ENTERS THE STAGE BEYOND THE SPOTLIGHT.

RHSO GUARD
(SHOUTING WHILST BEATING
A GARBAGE CAN WITH A BATON)
Time to get up. Rise and shine, you blackguards.

RHSO GUARD EXITS. DIETRICH TRIES TO AWAKEN. HE SITS UP. A FEW FEET AWAY A SPOTLIGHT COMES UP ON A WEARY-

EYED KLAUS, ALSO SITTING, WAKING
UP AND FACING DIETRICH. KLAUS IS
ALSO IN PRISON UNIFORM.

DIETRICH

Klaus. Klaus. It's you.

KLAUS

None other.

DIETRICH
(REACHING INTO HIS BAG)

Are you hungry? All they have here for breakfast is
warmed up water.

(WITH BREAD IN HAND)

Here.

KLAUS

No.

DIETRICH

No?

KLAUS

It's too early for that.

DIETRICH

You were never one for breakfasts. Do you mind?

KLAUS SHAKES HIS HEAD. DIETRICH
BEGINS TO GNAW AT A PIECE OF BREAD.

DIETRICH

It's been almost two years, Klaus...at Dad's 75th birthday party. You can't imagine how delighted I am to see you, even here. Not that I ever wanted you in prison. Not that I'd want to be in prison.

KLAUS

But I'm here and you, too. Do you have any regrets?

DIETRICH

Not in coming back to Germany. It's what I had to do.

KLAUS

Operation U7 is when things began to unravel.

DIETRICH

Perhaps.

KLAUS

They should have been smuggled out, not sent to Switzerland as spies. That aroused the attention of the Gestapo and SS.

DIETRICH

There's nothing we can do about it now.

KLAUS

It was stupid.

DIETRICH

Let's forget that. I want to ask you to forgive me for however I've wronged you. I regret we haven't talked these last two years.

KLAUS

It doesn't matter.

DIETRICH

It does. Life is so short, so tumultuous. We're supposed to love one another despite the sin...

A MOAN IS HEARD.

DIETRICH
(CONTINUING)

and despite the din.

KLAUS

Funny.

ANOTHER MOAN IS HEARD.

DIETRICH

You'll find the black humor helps. God have mercy on us all.

KLAUS

Don't you ever regret having joined the Resistance? After all the attempts on Hitler's life, where did we get? In the end the Russians will be the one's who clean house in Berlin.

DIETRICH

I think God expected us to try to clean house. And we tried.

KLAUS

You act as if you were the puppet of a bloody god. Doesn't that ever seem a contradiction to your Christianity?

DIETRICH

It's not that way.

RHSO GUARD ENTERS STAGE TO
A SPOTLIT AREA. LIGHTS OUT ON KLAUS.

RHSO GUARD
(SHOUTING)

I said, time to get up, you blackguards!

DIETRICH REACHES OUT.

DIETRICH

Klaus, Klaus. My brother.

DIETRICH RUBS HIS EYES,
THEN REALIZES HE HAS HALLUCINATED.

RHSO GUARD
(SHOUTING)

Get your cups ready for morning soup, you miserable
swine.

LIGHTS OUT ON THE SET. THE
SOUNDTRACK OF A TRUCK MOTORING
ALONG, CHANGING GEARS, STOPPING,
AND RESUMING TRAVEL IS HEARD
AS THE STAGEHANDS PREPARE THE
SET FOR THE NEXT SCENE.
RHSO GUARD EXITS.

SCENE 2K

SETTING:

WE ARE AT THE CONCENTRATION CAMP IN FLOSSENBERG, IN APRIL 1945. TIER 1 ACTS AS THE CAMP'S OPEN GROUNDS. THE STAGE LEVEL ACTS AS A CELL BLOCK. IF THE PRODUCTION PERMITS, THE IMAGE OF A GUARD TOWER CAN FORM PART OF THE BACKDROP; SUGGESTIONS OF BARBED WIRE MAY FESTOON THE SET.

AT RISE:

AS THE LIGHTS COME UP ON TIER 1, DIETRICH AND CANARIS ARE BROUGHT ON CLUTCHING BAGS OF THE SORT FIRST SEEN IN THE PREVIOUS SCENE. THEY ARE IN THE CUSTODY OF CAMP GUARDS 1 AND 2, IN SS UNIFORM. UNDER A LIGHT, ULRICH, IN A GESTAPO OFFICER'S UNIFORM, IS PERUSING A CLIPBOARDED REPORT. THE REPORT OF DISTANT CANNONADE IS HEARD FROM TIME TO TIME IN THIS AND FOLLOWING SCENES.

CAMP GUARD 1
Here are the last two traitors, sir.

ULRICH
Prisoner Canaris.

CANARIS
Here.

ULRICH
Take him away.

CAMP GUARD 2 AND
CANARIS EXIT STAGE.

ULRICH
Prisoner Bonhoeffer.

DIETRICH
Ah...here.

ULRICH
You needn't be familiar.

DIETRICH
After all this time, the admonitions haven't changed. Neither yours, nor will mine...sir.

A CANNON SHOT IS HEARD.

ULRICH
Guard, you are dismissed.

CAMP GUARD 1 DOESN'T LEAVE.

ULRICH
Yes, you are dismissed. I will take the prisoner to his hut.

CAMP GUARD 1
Yes, sir.

CAMP GUARD 1 EXITS.

DIETRICH
Such a long time since we first met in Wedding. I hope your family are well enough in the chaos.

ULRICH
Worry about yourself. Group Leader Sonderkothen, himself, will arrive in a few hours to conduct the trials ordered for you, Canaris, and four others.

DIETRICH
Still kicking around is he?

A CANNON SHOT IS HEARD.

ULRICH
What do you mean by that?

DIETRICH
I can hear the American cannons to the west. With the Americans, Brits, and French from the west and the Russians from the east I would say this and every other German death camp will soon be out of business. You must be concerned.

ULRICH

I've only been directly associated with the camps for the past month.

DIETRICH

Does it salve your conscience you've been associated with the intake rather than the discharge side of the machinery of death?

ULRICH

I could kill you on the spot for a remark like that.

DIETRICH

The child of God in you is not yet dead.

ULRICH
(PAUSE)

I wanted to tell you I'm sorry it's come to this.

DIETRICH

You shouldn't have joined them. But I suppose that's a silly remark.

ULRICH

Yes, look who's talking.

DIETRICH

There are good and bad reasons for joining anything, good or bad. There are almost always good reasons for doing bad things. That helps make evil so evil. The power to discern good and simultaneously do evil may as much derive from our wooden heads as it does from our wooden hearts. Have you thought about that? The less we pray the more wooden our heads and hearts become.

ULRICH

You haven't lost your desire to teach.

DIETRICH

That's because God hasn't lost his desire to love you. He never does. We're in Eastertide now. It's a good time to start listening to God again. His Spirit helps overcome our woodeness.

ULRICH

I've never quite made you out. I know you must be angry about my Party membership, yet you provide advice as if I were a friend.

DIETRICH

We must judge deeds, but it is not ours to judge the man or woman. God frees us to be brothers and sisters—always.

ULRICH

Group Leader Sonderkothen will be here to judge you, not to befriend you.

DIETRICH

I don't deny the necessity of legal judgment. It's a blessing when the laws attempt to reflect the laws of God.

ULRICH

You shouldn't have joined the Resistance.

DIETRICH

Some things done are past recovery.

(PAUSE)

How is your wife? I wish I had met her at some point. It always helps if you can picture someone when you pray for them.

ULRICH
We have a boy now.

DIETRICH
A boy! What a blessing! Congratulations! I must confess I wish I had had a family and children. That's more of an Old Testament wish than a New Testament one, but then the God of both is the God of all. How old is your boy?

ULRICH
Two weeks.

DIETRICH
Two weeks! Have you seen him? Where are your wife and boy?

ULRICH
In a small town just west of Berlin.

DIETRICH
I will pray for them both.

ULRICH
Yes, please do.

DIETRICH
It would help to know their names.

ULRICH
My wife is Anna. She and I disagree on his name, so he doesn't have one yet.

DIETRICH

You'd better do something about that.

ULRICH

She wants the name Alfred; I've always said I've wanted the name Adolf.

DIETRICH

She's thinking ahead. But I have another name to offer up, for several reasons: Andreas.

ULRICH

Andreas. Why Andreas?

DIETRICH

Saint Andreas, the brother of Saint Peter, was the first to follow Christ, yet our Lord gave Peter precedence. Another child was given to you in precedence to your boy just born, yet this boy can also be a first in your family— a first to be raised in the way of Christ. Give him the name Andreas to signal this new commitment to our Lord. Raise him as a Christian. With the name Andreas you would also be honoring...

CAMP GUARD 1 ENTERS.

ULRICH

Prisoner to attention.

DIETRICH STANDS AT ATTENTION.

ULRICH
Escort Prisoner Bonhoeffer to his assigned area.

CAMP GUARD 1 AND DIETRICH
EXIT STAGE. ULRICH LOOKS AWAY.
A CANNONADE IS HEARD FOLLOWED
BY SNIPPETS OF A BBC BROADCAST,
CIRCA APRIL 1945. THE BBC
AUDIOCAST COVERS THE
PREPARATION OF THE NEXT SCENE.

SCENE 2L

SETTING:

WE ARE AT DIETRICH'S CELL AT THE FLOSSENBERG CONCENTRATION CAMP, 9 APRIL 1945, FOLLOWING THE SS TRIAL. A CRUDE BUNK BED ON THE STAGE LEVEL IS BATHED IN A POOL OF LIGHT. THE REMAINDER OF THE SET SHOULD BE DARK, EXCEPT FOR SMALL SPOTS OF LIGHT SERVING AS A PATHWAY BETWEEN THE BUNK BED AND THE POINT OF ENTRY AND EXIT ON STAGE LEFT. A SLIVER OF BLUE LIGHT MAY APPEAR ABOVE TIER 2, TO REPRESENT THE COMING DAWN.

AT RISE:

AS THE LIGHTS COME UP, DIETRICH IS LED BY CAMP GUARDS 2 AND 3 FROM STAGE LEFT TO THE BUNK. ULRICH ENTERS FROM STAGE LEFT JUST AS DIETRICH IS DELIVERED TO HIS CELL. ULRICH RUSHES TO THE "DOOR" OF THE CELL. THE TWO CAMP GUARDS AND ULRICH EXCHANGE PERFUNCTORY, SILENT PARTY SALUTES AS THEY MEET EACH OTHER. CAMP GUARDS 2 AND 3 EXIT STAGE.

ULRICH

You were silent through your trial. Why didn't you speak up? Admiral Canaris's trial went on and on. You might have dragged things out, if you'd defended yourself.

DIETRICH

I would have if I'd had a trial.

ULRICH

In this world you can't expect to do things on your own terms.

DIETRICH

How true. But that is as He would have it.

ULRICH

He? God? You were the one who decided to come back to this country.

DIETRICH

And I thank God I returned.

ULRICH

Should we thank Him for the bombings and armies that are destroying Germany?

DIETRICH

Those things are signs of His wrath and His love. I thank Him that He has not abandoned us to our blindness or tyranny.

ULRICH

Always so ready with the defense of God. I've never known when it is *you* who are speaking.

DIETRICH

You need to hear God, first. He doesn't want to let you go.

ULRICH

You are nothing but a puppet for God. You are nothing. You are nothing! How can I want to be like you if you are nothing? I could admire you if you had defended yourself. But you didn't have the desire of Canaris to live nor the pride to defend your actions. Can't you see why I've never been able to commit myself to your Jesus Christ? Christianity is a form of self-annihilation. I won't have it.

DIETRICH

Then why are you here?

ULRICH

To tell you they have ordered me to conduct your hanging.

DIETRICH

Do they know you were a student of mine?

ULRICH

Yes. They've known for years.

DIETRICH

Are you going to do it?

ULRICH

Not doing it means throwing out the window all that I became in the New Order. I wanted the New Order to succeed. It seemed like the best chance we ever had of purging Western Civilization of the evils corrupting it.

DIETRICH

By modern definition I am part of the corruption. And yet I think you're reluctant to participate in my hanging. Am I right?

ULRICH

I shouldn't be. You're more robot, more puppet than you are human. Why is it that you always talk of Christ?

DIETRICH

With friends and family and all the acquaintances that I made in prison, I could talk of other things because I was not at war. With you and your associates I felt I was always in battle, so I raised the banner of faith—for my sake and yours. Perhaps I should have put the banner down long ago, for your sake, and Christ's. Forgive me.

ULRICH

There you go again. Couldn't you show some sign you don't accept what's coming to you? Show some sign of your humanity! Be angry at me; be angry at God!

DIETRICH

I thank God anger is a stranger to me.

ULRICH

Oh, yes, thank God for that.

DIETRICH
(ENDING WITH A LAUGH)

But I've often enough been frightened. And now I'm sad, if that's any consolation.

(PAUSE)

What a wonderful gift is life, even with another life in the offing. It looks as if there'll be a bright day ahead. One of my brothers, Karl-Frederich—you've met him —, once listed off good things in this life and he could have gone on and on there are so many good things. The one I most wanted—a wife and family of my own—didn't make my brother's list or my God's. But so be it; I'm thankful for the blessings I've had.

ULRICH

You talk as if your life were over. I'll get you out of here, Pastor. I can't hang you.

DIETRICH

God bless you, but escape is out of the question now. Anything impulsive would be suicidal. You know that.

ULRICH ACKNOWLEDGES THE TRUTH OF THAT WITH HEAD AND BODY.

DIETRICH

There is a time and season for everything under the sun. Everywhere, now and through eternity, there is movement, dance, song, thanks be to God. God holds us with His hands but moves us with His love. He asks that you love, too, for then you will have life.

(BRIEF PAUSE)

I think it is God's will that you move on. Forgive me for not being a better student of yours. I forgive you for not being a better student of mine. You'd better go while you can.

CAMP GUARDS 1 AND 2 ENTER.

ULRICH

Pastor.

DIETRICH

Repent and serve God.

ULRICH

I don't know what to say.

DIETRICH

Go, turn quickly. In Christ's name, remember me to your Anna...and to Andreas.

ULRICH EXITS STAGE, MEETING
THE CAMP GUARDS AS THEY
WALK TO DIETRICH'S CELL.

CAMP GUARD 1

Prisoner, strip off your clothes for the People's Sacrifice!

CAMP GUARD 2

We don't want any of your shit!

CAMP GUARDS 1 AND 2 LAUGH.
DIETRICH BEGINS TO REMOVE HIS
SHOES AND CLOTHES DOWN TO HIS
UNDERWEAR AS THE CAMP GUARDS
SMIRK AND GLARE AT HIM. THE
LIGHTS GO DOWN ON THE SET. THE
TWITTER OF A BIRD IS HEARD.

SCENE 2M

SETTING:

WE ARE AT THE EXECUTION AREA IN THE FLOSSENBERG CONCENTRATION CAMP ON 9 APRIL 1945 JUST AFTER DAWN. PART OF A GALLOWS MAY BE SEEN ON TIER 2, STAGE RIGHT. THE SAFFRON TWILIGHT IS JUST PAST AND EARLY DAYLIGHT FILTERS THROUGH TREES, AS MUCH AS CAN BE SUGGESTED.

AT RISE:

AS THE LIGHT COMES UP ON THE STAGE SET, DIETRICH IS KNEELING IN PRAYER IN THE CENTER OF THE STAGE LEVEL. DIETRICH HAS NOTHING ON BUT HIS UNDERPANTS; HE SHIVERS FROM TIME TO TIME. STANDING NEAR HIM BUT WITH HIS BACK TO THE AUDIENCE IS CAMP GUARD 3, RELATIVELY RELAXED (AND PERHAPS SMOKING A CIGARETTE). CAMP GUARDS 1 AND 2 ARE ON TIER 2, PREPARING TO CARRY OFF THE VIRTUALLY NAKED BODY OF CANARIS. (A STRETCHER MAY ABET THIS TASK.)

SONDERKOTHEN ENTERS IN SS UNIFORM
BUT BEREFT OF HIS CAP. HE IS HOLDING
A RIDING CROPPER. HE IS ESCORTED BY
CAMP GUARD 4. CAMP GUARD 3
SNAPS TO ATTENTION. THE SOUND
OF A CANNONADE IS HEARD.

SONDERKOTHEN
So the work is not yet finished.

CAMP GUARD 2
We're ready to take this one off to the ovens.

SONDERKOTHEN
Don't take it to the ovens. Hand it off to the duty
sergeant's team and get right back here.

CAMP GUARD 2
Yes, sir.

CAMP GUARDS 1 AND 2 BEGIN WALKING
DOWN FROM TIER 2 TO TIER 1, CARRYING
THE BODY OF CANARIS. SONDERKOTHEN
WALKS TO MEET THEM, ESCORTED
BY CAMP GUARD 4.

SONDERKOTHEN
And this is our late loyal Admiral Canaris.

(AT FIRST LOOKING OVER CANARIS'S BODY)
Et tu, Bruté. Get this bag of vomit out of my sight and get
back here so that we can take care of the last one.

CAMP GUARDS 1 AND 2

Yes, sir.

CAMP GUARDS 1 AND 2 EXIT.
SONDERKOTHEN APPROACHES DIETRICH.

SONDERKOTHEN
(BRUSHING DIETRICH WITH HIS RIDING CROPPER)

What is the meaning of this?

DIETRICH CROSSES HIMSELF AND
THEN, STILL ON HIS KNEES,
LOOKS UP AT SONDERKOTHEN.

DIETRICH
(QUIETLY)

I am praying, sir.

SONDERKOTHEN

I know that and, as I've said, God is beyond listening. Yet as a representative of modernity I have an interest in everything that takes place in *this* world. I'm just curious what you're praying about.

DIETRICH

There's much I've been praying about.

SONDERKOTHEN

I would think your own soul, as you call it, would be of first importance. Am I not right?

DIETRICH

No. I rely on Christ's mercy to take care of me. But I was thanking Him and praying for others. And for forgiveness.

SONDERKOTHEN

You just don't know when to quit, do you? You're going to be on the butterfly trap in minutes. For once before you die, be a man. Be honest...if that is possible. How can you thank any god for what's happened to you? Aren't you really afraid to admit you were the angel of your own death?

CAMP GUARDS 1 AND 2 ENTER.

DIETRICH

I'm not afraid to take responsibility. I am proud to have served Christ...and as a German.

SONDERKOTHEN

Liar! Your god is a lie; Jesus Christ is a lie; and you're a liar and a traitor.

DIETRICH

God forgive us all.

SONDERKOTHEN
(STRIKING DIETRICH)

Shut up!

(BRIEF PAUSE)

And to think my colleagues believed you were a fool, just because you were so straightforwardly anti-Party. I almost fell for that, too. But something told me there was more to you than pure innocence. And I was right. You are a lizard, a snake. No, worse than a snake. A dinosaur, full of medieval vomit. Your treachery was all the more dangerous because you seemed to be just a museum piece. You seemed harmless. A new civilization will yet arise that will give you and your kind and your lies an exit ticket to eternity. The end of religious delusions will be like a breath of fresh air for all who are worthy of life.

(BRIEF PAUSE)
Take him to the ticket window.

CAMP GUARD 1
Stand up, you turd bucket!

CAMP GUARD 2
Put your hands up!

DIETRICH PUTS HIS HANDS IN FRONT
OF HIMSELF FORMING WITH EACH
HAND THE "HAND KISS" TAUGHT HIM
BY MARIA. HE BEGINS TO BRING
THE HANDS TOGETHER.

CAMP GUARD 1
(GRABBING DIETRICH)
You idiot!

CAMP GUARD 2
Not in front; in back, like the others, you dumb puppet.

SONDERKOTHEN
I want cooperation or you'll be hanging from piano wire for hours.

DIETRICH NODS HIS HEAD IN ASSENT.
THE GUARDS TIE DIETRICH'S HANDS
BEHIND HIS BACK. THE SOUND OF
A CANNONADE IS HEARD.

SONDERKOTHEN

Where is Lieutenant Schmidt?

CAMP GUARD 2

I asked for him when we delivered the Admiral's body. They don't know where he is.

SONDERKOTHEN
(TO CAMP GUARD 3)

Go and notify the guards. Schmidt is to be shot on sight for being absent without permission. Go! Go!

CAMP GUARD 3 EXITS. GUARDS 1 AND 2
MOVE DIETRICH ALONG BRISKLY
TO THE GALLOWS. DIETRICH
OFFERS NO RESISTANCE.

SONDERKOTHEN
(TO CAMP GUARD 4)

The corruption! And so little time to put it out. If there were a god who acted in history it wouldn't be so difficult for modern man.

CAMP GUARDS 1 AND 2 TAKE DIETRICH
TO THE GALLOWS, PRESUMABLY JUST
OFF STAGE FROM TIER 2, STAGE RIGHT.
SONDERKOTHEN AND CAMP GUARD 4
ARE WATCHING THEM.

A DISTANT CANNON SHOT IS HEARD.

SONDERKOTHEN

Are you ready?

CAMP GUARD 1

It is ready, sir.

SONDERKOTHEN

Bonhoeffer, you won't wriggle out of this one. Make the angel writhe for his ticket, men. I want a "religious experience."

CAMP GUARD 1

Now, sir?

SONDERKOTHEN

Do it!

CAMP GUARD 1

Yes, sir.

SONDERKOTHEN ARCHES BACK
HIS HEAD. AS HE BECOMES SATISFIED
THAT THE NOOSE IS TAKING HOLD ON
BONHOEFFER, HE SMILES. THEN HE
RESUMES AN ERECT POSTURE.

SONDERKOTHEN

Is he dead already?

CAMP GUARD 1
He must be. He's not moving.

SONDERKOTHEN
That was quick.

A CANNONADE IS HEARD.

CAMP GUARD 1
The oven'll finish him off, sir, if there's a breath left.

SONDERKOTHEN
You're right. Cut the purple wretch down. At least we can now report to Berlin—it is finished.

CAMP GUARDS 1 AND 2 PROCEED TO REMOVE DIETRICH'S BODY FROM THE NOOSE. SONDERKOTHEN RAPIDLY EXITS STAGE LEFT. THE CAMP GUARDS PROCEED TO FOLLOW WITH DIETRICH'S BODY, ALBEIT SLOWLY. THE COO OF A MOURNING DOVE IS HEARD. ONE OF THE CAMP GUARDS, STARTLED, LOOKS BRIEFLY FOR THE BIRD, AS THE GUARDS PROCEED. THE GUARDS EXIT. THE DOVE IS HEARD TWICE MORE AS THE LIGHTS FADE DOWN ON THE SET.

CURTAIN DOWN. WITH THE CURTAIN CALL, RESOUND "FOR ALL THE SAINTS." THIS HYMN WAS SUNG AT THE MEMORIAL SERVICE FOR DIETRICH BONHOEFFER HELD IN JULY 1945 AT HOLY TRINITY

CHURCH, KINGSWAY, LONDON, A SERVICE BROADCAST BY THE BBC. DIETRICH'S PARENTS TUNED INTO THE BBC JUST AS THE HYMN WAS BEING AIRED. THEY LEARNED OF THEIR SON'S DEATH AS THE BROADCAST CONTINUED. IN THE CLOSING DAYS OF THE WAR DIETRICH'S PARENTS ALSO LOST TO THE MACHINERY OF VENGEANCE THEIR SON KLAUS AND THEIR SONS-IN-LAW HANS VON DOHNANYI AND RUDIGER SCHLEICHER.

<u>END OF PLAY</u>

Printed in the United States
82601LV00002B/211-219/A